THE BEST
INDIAN
PEAKS
WILDERNESS
HIKES

JAMES DZIEZYNSKI

The Colorado Mountain Club Press
Golden, Colorado

The Best Indian Peaks Wilderness Hikes
© 2019 by Colorado Mountain Club Press

PUBLISHED BY

The Colorado Mountain Club Press
710 Tenth Street, Suite 200
Golden, Colorado 80401
303-996-2743 email: cmcpress@cmc.org   website: CMC.org

Founded in 1912, the Colorado Mountain Club is the largest outdoor recreation, education and conservation organization in the Rocky Mountains.

CONTACTING THE PUBLISHER
We appreciate readers alerting us to any errors or outdated information at the above address.

James Dziezynski author, photographer unless noted otherwise
Takeshi Takahashi: design, composition, and production
Mira Perrizo: editor
Clyde Soles: publisher

DISTRIBUTED TO THE BOOK TRADE BY
Mountaineers Books, 1001 Klickitat Way, Suite 201, Seattle, WA 98134, 800-553-4453, Mountaineersbooks.org

COVER PHOTO:
The traverse between Mount Neva and Mount Jasper.

We gratefully acknowledge the financial support of the people of Colorado through the Scientific and Cultural Facilities District of greater Denver for our publishing activities.

TOPOGRAPHIC MAPS were created using CalTopo.com.

WARNING: Hiking and climbing are high-risk activities. This guidebook is not a substitute for experience, training, and common sense. The users of this guidebook assume full responsibility for their own safety. Weather, terrain conditions, and individual experience and abilities must be considered before undertaking any of the outings in this guide. The Colorado Mountain Club and the author do not assume any liability for injury, death, damage to property, or violation of the law that may result from the use of this book

Printed in Korea.

ISBN: 978-1-937052-68-3

Looking south to 13,368' Engelmann Peak from Colorado Mines Peak.

CONTENTS

ACKNOWLEDGMENTS

I am extremely grateful for the friends with whom I've had the privilege of sharing mountain adventures. Big thanks to my wife Sheila and our pups Mystic and Fremont. Also thanks to Jon Bradford, Janet Seston, Paul Lenhart, David Tanguay, Daniela Tanguay, Meredith Knauf, Debbie Bruggeman, Jayme Moye, Doug Schnitzspahn, Bart Deferme, Tracy Zedeck, Lindsey Tate, Marie Willson, Becky Pahl, Jenny Salentine, Clyde Soles, and Shaine Smith.

Mount Neva's incredible north ridge.

En route to the summit of Mount Audubon.

Gourd Lake on a perfect summer day.

Introduction

INDIAN PEAKS WILDERNESS

The 76,711 acres that make up the Indian Peaks Wilderness (IPW) can satisfy a lifetime of adventure. Summits over 13,000 feet rise from the plains and foothills to the east, announcing the Rocky Mountains in spectacular style. Sparkling lakes, jagged spires, rounded summit domes, sprawling forests, and hardy glaciers are just some of the natural features that make this one of Colorado's—and America's—premier alpine settings. Wildflowers paint the land in vibrant colors in spring while winter's frozen palette summons hidden beauty for those daring enough to seek it out.

Designated in 1978, the Indian Peaks Wilderness is made up of many worlds. Erosion and glacial transformation are delightfully inconsistent, resulting in friendly, walk-up summits and frightfully exposed technical ridges. The last remaining glaciers that shaped the land over thousands of years are retreating, shadows of their once imperial power to alter the land. Clear alpine pools and dozens of surprisingly large lakes decorate the drainages and high basins that skirt some of Colorado's most amazing mountains. A rich diversity of wildlife from the mighty moose to the mischievous marmot call this region home and some of the toughest locals—such as pika and ptarmigan—remain at the highest elevations year-round.

Because it is one of the closest high-mountain ranges to the Denver/Boulder metro area, the IPW can be a busy place. The easily accessed portals of the Brainard Lake Recreation Area and the Hessie trailhead offer instant alpine gratification in the form of gorgeous mountain views, lakes that are mere feet from parking lots, and even curious wildlife. Destinations east of the Continental Divide (that runs north-south through the Wilderness) are the most popular, though there are still many secrets waiting to be found.

The western IPW is a very different character. While the eastern IPW has many well-developed trails going to its most popular lakes and summits, the Wilderness Area west of the Divide is more primitive. Access routes tend to spend more time in the forests, trails are less traveled, wildlife is a little more at home, and summits (especially those under 13,000 feet) are lonely places.

This contrast makes the IPW appealing to all visitors. Those looking for an easy outing to a beautiful area that is safe and well-developed but still naturally intact can enjoy places like Long Lake, Brainard Lake, and Blue Lake. Those yearning for isolation can range out to remote summits like Hiamovi Mountain and Watanga Mountain. Thrill-seekers can challenge the daring traverse of the Arapaho Peaks or the rugged summit of Navajo Peak.

Hessie Trailhead Shuttle

Boulder County and RTD began a shuttle service to the popular Hessie trailhead to minimize traffic and give hikers access to the trailhead, which has limited parking. The shuttle runs on weekends and holidays from late May to early October. Normal operating hours are 8:00 am–8:00 pm Saturdays, 8:00 am–6:00 pm Sundays from May to September; in October both weekend days run 8:00 am–6:00 pm. The shuttle also runs on Memorial Day, the 4th of July, and Labor Day if those days happen to fall on weekdays.

Grab the shuttle at Nederland's RTD Park-n-Ride at the intersection of 1st and Jackson Streets, just off the Peak-to-Peak Highway (CO-72) when you first enter town. There is plenty of free parking here. Shuttles run every 15–20 minutes and leashed dogs are welcome. For more info visit www.hessietrailhead.com or call 303-441-1032.

JAMES PEAK WILDERNESS

Established in 2002, the tastefully named James Peak Wilderness (JPW) is a fine counterpart to the Indian Peaks Wilderness. At 17,015 acres, it's smaller than the IPW but packs a lot of adventure in that space. The connecting ridge that spans north-south through the Wilderness contains five 13,000-foot peaks, all of them gracefully smoothed by centuries of glacial erosion. Human history is rich in the JPW, including the world's highest non-cog railroad, once located atop Rollins Pass and the more recently extinct boundary of the Berthoud Pass Ski area.

Combined, these two Wilderness Areas are pure Colorado. Despite lacking one of the state's wildly popular 14,000-foot summits, visitors will soon learn that size isn't everything. Adventures large and small await among the ancient landscape and modern trails. This guide is your gateway to the very best of these adventures.

Hiking back from Hidden Point near Berthoud Pass.

Using This Guide

RATINGS

Difficulty ratings in this guide are **relative to the type of terrain found in the Wilderness Areas.** While there is an assumption of a decent level of base-fitness, difficulty ratings are impossible to define using average-human fitness (especially in Colorado, where super-athletes abound).

Also: all routes in the book are considered non-technical, in that the standard routes do not require ropes, climbing shoes, and technical climbing gear. However, there are a few optional routes or moves where a rope is completely acceptable, though many climbers usually do not bring them. These are well described in their respective chapters. With that in mind:

Easy: Easy hikes are done on-trail or with very, very simple off-trail navigation. The challenge of route-finding is mostly out of your hands. The footing is good, though there may be respectable changes in elevation—remember, you are in the Rocky Mountains and mountains tend to go uphill!

Moderate: These routes offer challenges in the form of distance, elevation gain, modest off-trail navigation, and

Diamond Lake. PHOTO BY DEBBI BRUGGEMAN

Sawtooth Mountain's impressive profile.

occasional route finding. Some easy scrambling may be required and the better your fitness, the easier Moderate hikes are.

Difficult: Difficult hikes are geared toward experienced mountain travelers with very good off-trail skills, good route finding ability, and better-than-average fitness. Scrambles may require a few skilled moves with exposure and some fall consequences. New and casual mountain hikers should work up to difficult hikes or team up with more experienced people.

Most Difficult: This designation is reserved for a very few routes, such as the Arapaho Peaks Traverse and Mount Neva's North Ridge. These adventures require strong route finding ability, confidence on exposed scrambling and climbing sections, excellent fitness, and strong mountain savvy in terms of reading rock, weather, and conditions.

THE CLASS SYSTEM

The class system is a way to designate the terrain difficulty on a given route assuming normal, dry conditions. Ratings can be subjective—a certain move deemed Class 3 by a 6'4" friend was easily Class 4 for your 5'8" author. In this guide, I err on the side of caution of overrating a move vs. underrating, for obvious reasons.

Class 1: Easy terrain with excellent footing, usually this refers to well-maintained trails, but some tundra walks with no obstacles can be considered Class 1. Note that Class 1 terrain does not heavily consider elevation gain, so Class 1 trails can still be work.

Class 2: Colorado's typical hiking trails fall into this category, as does off-trail terrain that does not require scrambling or extended use of the hands. Trails can be rocky and off-camber. Off-trail terrain includes boulder fields, scree slopes, and loose gullies that aren't overly steep.

Class 3: Class 3 terrain often requires scrambling on solid hand-and-foot holds. Class 3 terrain can almost always be reversed mid-move, either by putting your butt or belly down or simply backing off. Class 3 terrain may have terrific exposure but is defined by the safety of the terrain you're actually on. That said, Class 3 terrain can be described as low-risk, low-to-medium consequence in case of a slip or fall. Some Class 3 downclimbs are best done face-in.

Mount Toll from Blue Lake. PHOTO BY DEBBI BRUGGEMAN

Snow can visit the Rocky Mountains any month of the year.

Class 4: Perhaps the most debated class, Class 4 is defined by low-risk, high-consequence moves. Scrambling or climbing is required on solid rock, though a fall on these moves could cause serious injury or death. Exposure is often very high and may be sustained on a route. Some climbers opt to take ropes on Class 4 routes, trading speed for safety.

Class 5: Technical climbing. There are no Class 5 routes in this guide. Class 5 routes require vertical or near-vertical climbing and most often is done with climbing equipment, free-solo climbers being the exception.

Weather and Altitude

Weather is king in Colorado, though it is often predictable. In prime hiking season (June—September), afternoon thunderstorms are practically guaranteed, even if they aren't in the forecast. Getting off all summits by 1:00 pm at the latest used to be a rule of thumb, but my personal rule is 11:30 am unless the forecast is absolutely clear (more likely in the shoulder seasons or winter). I like to be on the trail no later than 6:00

Open tundra en route to Hiamovi Mountain, one of the gems of the western Indian Peaks.

am, unless it's a quick summit or a hike that never goes above treeline.

Weather is no joke in Colorado, and that applies to the IPW and JPW areas. Storms can form from clear blue skies in less than 20 minutes and getting trapped above treeline is a dangerous and harrowing experience. Read forecasts before your hike, get out there early, and remain vigilant.

Altitude is another concern, especially for out-of-state visitors. While many destinations in this guide are "only" 11,000 feet or lower, that's still enough to bring on altitude sickness in the form of a lingering headache, upset stomach, dizziness, shortness of breath, and nausea. It's normal to get a little winded at altitude, but if you (or your hiking partner) starts to seem lethargic, cranky, and fatigued, it is best to turn around. Stress and poor sleep can promote altitude sickness even in local Coloradans.

Staying hydrated is important, as is setting a pace that doesn't fizzle you out before you've even left treeline. Knowing thyself and thy friends is a huge advantage to recognizing altitude sickness.

OTHER SAFETY CONCERNS AND GOOD FORM IN THE MOUNTAINS

- Bring along enough food and hydration for your hike (3 liters of water is a safe margin).

- First-aid kits should always be in your pack—including first-aid gear for your dogs if needed.

- Navigational tools should always be in your pack as well. I'm a big fan of GPS and GPS apps, but I also am skilled at map and compass reading (and carry them on all hikes).

- Bring sunblock and invest in a good pair of protective sunglasses.

- Bring layers for all conditions at any time of the year. This includes warm, non-cotton base layers, jackets, and rain shells. Hats, gloves, dry socks, and puffy jackets should also be in your pack. Colorado weather can change in a flash, even on the warmest summer day.

- Always have a headlamp or flashlight with charged batteries in your pack. Always!

- Do not let your dogs chase wildlife. Colorado's mountains have moose, black bears, mountain lions, and mountain goats—all of which have no problem counter-attacking your dog if provoked. Likewise, porcupine, badgers, and even marmots can cause serious injury to your dog.

Shoshoni Peak's "crow's nest" summit block.

- Colorado wildlife is just that: wild. Leave them be and get out of their way. The IPW, in particular, has seen an explosion in the moose population, and these powerful ungulates are not to be trifled with. Give them space and if they start chomping or doing their "river dance" with their forelegs, do not make eye contact and slowly back off. Get your dogs leashed immediately!

- Yield to uphill hikers as a general rule. The exception I make is when backpackers are coming downhill and I'm hiking or it's a technical section where it's simply easier for me as the uphill hiker to step off the trail.

- Be nice to other hikers, even if you're having a crummy day.

- Leave No Trace ethics (pack it out, leave nature as you found it) are required.

- Cell phones often don't work up here. Consider carrying an emergency locator device such as the Garmin inReach. These are excellent investments, even if you never personally have to use them—you may be able to help another hiker in distress.

- Finally, invest in a Colorado CORSAR card. It's dirt cheap—$3 for a one-year card or $12 for a 5-year card. This card helps offset the cost to you in case of a search and rescue. If you never need it (which hopefully is the case) the funding supports Colorado Search and Rescue Teams. Pick one up here: dola.colorado.gov/sar/cardPurchase.jsf

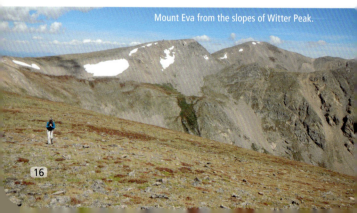

Mount Eva from the slopes of Witter Peak.

Snowy spring views from Mount Flora.

Wilderness Regulations and Rules

The complete set of rules and regulations are available from the US Forest Service. Search fs.usda.gov for the relevant web pages.

For information on permits, conditions, and other information, contact:

USFS Boulder Ranger District

> 2140 Yarmouth Avenue
> Boulder, CO 80301
> 303-541-2500

USFS Sulphur Ranger District

> 9 Ten Mile Drive
> P.O. Box 10
> Granby, CO 80446
> 970-887-4100

USFS Clear Creek Ranger District

> @ Idaho Springs Visitors Center
> 2060 Miner Street
> Idaho Springs, CO 80452
> 303-567-4382

Here are the most relevant rules and regulations in the Indian Peaks Wilderness (IPW) and the James Peak Wilderness (JPW).

- Pets must be on a hand-held leash at all times.

More James Peak Wilderness beauty.

- JPW: Camping is allowed without a permit. Campsites must be 100 feet away from lakes, rivers, and streams. Campfires are prohibited but camp stoves are allowed. Camp group size is limited to 12 people.

- IPW: There are many campground camping options in the IPW, which include: Pawnee Campground, Rainbow Lakes Campground, Kelly Dahl Campground, Camp Dick Campground, and Peaceful Valley Campground east of the Continental Divide, and Big Rock Campground, Moraine Campground, and Arapaho Bay Campground west of the Divide. Please contact the above Ranger Districts for current fees, reservations, and seasonality.

- IPW: Backcountry Camping is a popular activity in the IPW. The regulations around backcountry camping are as follows:

  June 1–September 15: Backcountry permits are required for all backcountry trips. As of 2019, this is a mere $5. Camping zones are divided into four backcountry districts and reservations must be made in advance at one of the ranger stations listed above. Make your reservations early—they fill up fast.

  Camping is prohibited in the Four Lakes Backcountry Zone from May 1–November 30. September 16–May 31: Permits are not required, but all other regulations remain in effect.

- IPW: No public access is allowed in the designated City of Boulder Watershed, with a few exceptions: South Arapaho Peak's summit, North Arapaho Peak's summit, Navajo Peak's summit, and parts of the Arapaho Glacier Trail. Leave No Trace ethics apply to both Wilderness Areas. Certain trailheads have parking fees. These are mentioned when applicable in each chapter.

1. St. Vrain Mountain and Meadow Mountain

RATING	Easy to Moderate
ROUND-TRIP DISTANCE	8.4 miles
ROUND-TRIP TIME	5–7 hours
ELEVATION GAIN	3,250 feet
MAP	Trails Illustrated #102, Indian Peaks, Gold Hill; Latitude 40° Maps - Boulder County, Front Range
NEAREST LANDMARK	Allenspark

COMMENT: Nestled in the northeast corner of the Indian Peaks Wilderness, this mountain hike is a great way to experience the peace, beauty, and elegance of the Rocky Mountains. Many Colorado treks shine in the autumn but the St. Vrain Trail is exceptionally gorgeous, thanks to its many aspen stands and expansive views into the deepest part of the southern portion of Rocky Mountain National Park. A side trip to Meadow Mountain (11,632 feet) crosses into Rocky Mountain National Park, a perfectly legal side trip.

St. Vrain Mountain (12,162 feet) is one of the most accessible summits in the northern Indian Peaks and embodies

Open meadows lead the way to the summit of St. Vrain Mountain.

classic Colorado mountain hiking: forest terrain that passes above treeline, eventually exposing a vast and mountainous world. Don't miss this one!

As with many of the hikes in this guide, you don't need to tag the summits to get your fill of mountainous fun. The 6-mile out-and-back to the saddle is a great day out for more casual hikers. Want to get both summits? St. Vrain Mountain then Meadow Mountain is the logical way to do it. If you are curious where the St. Vrain Mountain Trail eventually goes, it descends south to Middle St. Vrain Creek and ends at the Buchanan Pass Trail.

St. Vrain Mountain is named for Ceran St. Vrain (1802–1870), a pioneer that established a trading company that served the region. In 1833, he helped create Bent's Fort, a hub for business between natives and settlers.

GETTING THERE: The St. Vrain Mountain trailhead is south of the tiny town of Allenspark off of Colorado Highway 7. Grab CO-7 in Lyons and follow it 18.5 miles. If coming from Estes Park in the north, take CO-7 for 15.5 miles. Turn south into the signed turnoff for Allenspark (CO-7 Business), then take a left onto Ski Road/FR-107 shortly after entering the town. Stay on this dirt road as it climbs south out of town, passes through a few outlying cabins, and eventually reaches a signed junction in about 1.6 miles. Turn right onto this switchbacking road and go 0.5 mile, where it will end at the trailhead. The road is suitable for all vehicles, though be aware of snow blocking the last 0.5-mile starting in early November.

There are only 7 parking spots in the main lot, but never fear, parking is available along the road. This trailhead is getting more popular every year, so please tread softly.

THE ROUTE: This trail starts in the Roosevelt National Forest east of the IPW boundary. Well-traveled and easy to follow, the St. Vrain Mountain Trail gradually climbs up to timberline at the saddle between Meadow Mountain and the shoulder of St. Vrain Mountain in 3.0 miles. Cross into the Indian Peaks Wilderness at 0.6 mile. Enjoy the walk up as

This is an excellent trail for autumn colors.

The saddle just after breaking treeline.

the trail nears a small creek before hitting a series of broad switchbacks at 10,000 feet.

At 3.0 miles in, views open up as you reach the saddle at 11,215 feet. This wide meadow has some of the most stunning views in Colorado: 13,176-foot Copeland Mountain looms large to the west, with Rocky Mountain National Park's southern peaks extending north to the well-known summit block of Longs Peak.

If you're looking to tag Meadow Mountain, it's 0.4 mile north along a social trail on easy slopes. Even though it's close to St. Vrain Mountain, the unique views from Meadow Mountain are distinct enough to warrant a visit. Also, if you're short on time or simply want a less strenuous day, this is a good option. If heading to St. Vrain Mountain, stay left (south) on the smooth St. Vrain Mountain Trail.

After 3.6 miles, revel in open meadows as you inadvertently pop in and out of the boundary of Rocky Mountain National Park. Waves of pine forests recede below and the icy portraits of the St. Vrain glaciers gradually come into view to the west. As you near the east slopes of St. Vrain Mountain, turn off the trail and head toward the highest point. There is no formal trail or sign, so pick a good spot to wander off-trail and hoof up 0.6 mile on good, open terrain to the summit. There is plenty of room to rest and relax on top. At 12,162 feet, it will seem like you're on a larger mountain. Views in all directions are wonderful and navigation back to the St. Vrain Mountain Trail is easy. When you're ready to return, go back the way you came.

THE BEST INDIAN PEAKS WILDERNESS HIKES

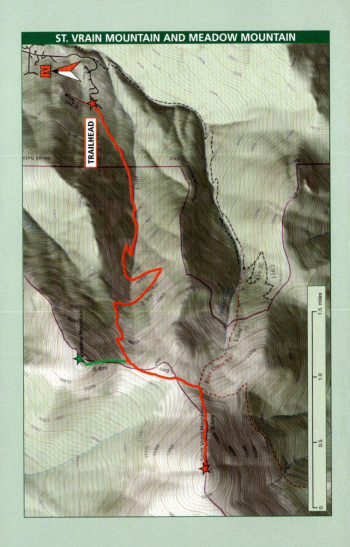

TRAILHEAD

2. Watanga Lake and Watanga Mountain

RATING	Watanga Lake, Moderate; Watanga Mountain, Moderate to Difficult
ROUND-TRIP DISTANCE	7.8 miles Watanga Lake; 11.6 miles Watanga Mountain
ROUND-TRIP TIME	5–7 hours Watanga Lake; 6–8 hours Watanga Mountain
ELEVATION GAIN	2,500 feet Watanga Lake; 4,120 feet Watanga Mountain
MAP	Trails Illustrated #102, Indian Peaks, Gold Hill; Latitude 40° Maps - Boulder County, Front Range
NEAREST LANDMARK	Lake Granby

NOTE: There is a $5 entrance fee for accessing the Roaring Fork trailhead

COMMENT: This show begins before you set foot on the Roaring Fork Trail (the main access point to Watanga Lake and Watanga Mountain). Drive along the shoreline and dams of Lake Granby en route to this lesser-known IPW trailhead. Fewer crowds and less development give the western side of the Wilderness a different vibe than the popular east side trails. Watanga Lake is a perfect example of the raw and pristine beauty of this hidden kingdom. Nestled below the hulking shoulder of Watanga Mountain, Watanga Lake (10,771 feet) has a well-maintained trail to a tiered alpine meadow featuring the eponymous lake.

Watanga Mountain (12,375 feet) ups the challenge by going off-trail through a small patch of easy-to-navigate woods, eventually connecting with the broad, moderate southwest slopes. Once established on these slopes, the walk up is an utter delight, ascending through wide-open tundra meadows, a humble boulder-strewn plateau, and even a thrilling micro-catwalk before topping out on one of the least visited

Peaceful pines surround Watanga Lake.

named summits in the Indian Peaks. For a modest day in the mountains, Watanga Lake is a fine goal. If you're wanting to go beyond the trail and explore some of the least-trodden ground in the IPW, Watanga Mountain is waiting.

Hiking poles are a very good idea for Watanga Mountain, specifically for the extended time you'll be spending on the southwest slopes. Looking west from Watanga Lake showcases the impressive face of Twin Peaks (11,957 feet), a summit that can be reached with some creative scrambling from the lake.

GETTING THERE: Follow US-34 north from the town of Granby. For Front Rangers, this means taking I-70 west to US-40 over Berthoud Pass and through the town of Winter Park. From the junction of US-40 and US-34, take US-34 for 5.4 miles and turn right onto CO-6. At the start of this road is a pay kiosk for the Arapaho National Recreation Area ($5 for day use as of 2019). Follow this impressive dirt road 8.8 miles along the southwest shore of Lake Granby, then take a left onto Highway 637 at the Big Rock Campground. Follow this road 0.8 mile farther to the Roaring Fork trailhead on your right. The trailhead is a roundabout with plenty of parking

The off-trail terrain en route to Watanga Mountain.

and is accessible to passenger cars. There is no additional fee to park here.

If coming from the Denver/Boulder metro area, this is a long drive—about 2 hours and 45 minutes. It may be worth reserving a site at one of the campgrounds in the area: Big Rock, Moraine, or Arapaho Bay. You can snag a site by visiting the Arapaho National Recreation Area (ANRA) website.

THE ROUTE: The Roaring Fork wastes no time in getting your heart pumping. After a stiff initial push, the grade eases as the trail cozies up to the Roaring Fork Arapaho Creek. Continue along this pleasant path for 2.4 miles to the junction with the Watanga Lake Trail. Take the left turnoff to the signed Watanga Lake Trail. Follow the trail as it crisscrosses Watanga Creek en route to Watanga Lake. If this is your goal for the day, enjoy the views from this tall grass–rimmed alpine pool and return the way you came, at your leisure. The mountainous wall on the east side of the lake is merely the shoulder of Watanga Mountain, whose summit is out of sight. If continuing on to the summit, prepare to go off-trail as you aim toward the southwest slopes.

Begin the trek to Watanga Peak by following a grassy passage on the south side of the lake. Above this is a tier of small ponds. There are excellent campsites throughout this swath of forest. Your goal is to gain the southwest slopes, which are in sight to your left. Rather than scramble up the steep, loose terrain immediately above the ponds, enjoy a pleasant off-trail walk southeast to a point where the slopes offer easier access. Staying slightly west (right of the ponds) through the woods offers nearly flat terrain and nice western views.

THE BEST INDIAN PEAKS WILDERNESS HIKES

Gaining the slopes at 4.4 miles looks intimidating from a distance, but keep an eye out for grassy access passages. With a bit of savvy navigating, getting onto the slopes will only require a brief, steep scramble (about 80 vertical feet). If using a GPS or map, it's a good idea to mark this spot so you can return the way you came—it may not be as obvious on the return. Once you gain the slope, turn uphill and enjoy the open terrain as you ascend. These slopes are broad, grassy, and have excellent footing. As the slopes become nearly flat before the top, it's unclear where the actual summit of Watanga Mountain is. Keep trending toward the highest point and don't stray too far left. You won't see the summit proper until you're nearly there. Just before reaching it, there's a very small "catwalk" (about 6 feet) that provides a cheap thrill before summiting. The highest point becomes obvious once past the catwalk.

Despite the relatively low elevation, don't be surprised if your legs feel shaky—you've come up over 4,000 vertical feet. If you're looking for the USGS survey marker, it's not on the actual summit. Rather, it's embedded in a boulder about 100 feet east of the summit, where the cracked southeast ridge joins the summit grounds. The descent back to Watanga Lake is straightforward as far as off-trail terrain goes, but make sure you don't walk past the turn off the shoulder back to the tiered ponds and eventually the lake. From the lake, you have the comforts of the Roaring Fork Trail to lead you back to the parking area.

3. Hiamovi Mountain and Mount Irving Hale

RATING	Hiamovi Mountain, Moderate to Difficult; Mount Irving Hale, Moderate to Difficult
ROUND-TRIP DISTANCE	10.2 miles Hiamovi Mountain; 8.9 miles Mount Irving Hale; 11.7 miles Hiamovi—Irving Hale Combo
ROUND-TRIP TIME	6–8 hours Hiamovi Mountain; 5–7 hours Mount Irving Hale; 7–9 hours Hiamovi—Irving Hale Combo
ELEVATION GAIN	4,080 feet Hiamovi Mountain; 3,480 feet Mount Irving Hale; 4,650 feet Hiamovi—Irving Hale Combo
MAPS	Trails Illustrated #102, Indian Peaks, Gold Hill; Latitude 40° Maps - Boulder County, Front Range
NEAREST LANDMARK	Lake Granby

COMMENT: Hiamovi Mountain (12,395 feet) and Mount Irving Hale (11,754) share a saddle off the Roaring Fork Trail, making them a nice pair to link up. Both require relatively straightforward off-trail navigation. With proper navigation, neither exceeds Class 2+ scrambling in difficulty. Half the challenge of these peaks is actually found on-trail, as the steep Roaring Fork Trail pushing nearly 3,000 vertical feet in under 4.0 miles—all before the work of reaching the summits begins. For fit hikers who are up to the call of the wild, these are two excellent summits in a remote part of the IPW.

Mount Irving Hale (8.9 miles round-trip) is a true hidden gem (I consider it a sister summit to Mount Epworth, page 101). After departing the Roaring Fork Trail, the route is a great intro to easy off-trail navigation. The final scramble to the summit is ridiculously fun, done on grippy, solid boulders with many short, unexposed Class 3–4 options to go along with the easiest line, a Class 2+ scramble. Summit views down to Lake Granby and the southern Indian Peaks are magnificent.

Hiamovi Mountain is a bit more work (10.2 miles round-trip). Climbers can boulder-hop up the southwest slopes or counter around to the west slopes, which are slightly more stable and less rock-strewn. En route is a very special place I've dubbed "Hiamovi Plateau." This flat, open, alpine meadow is a fine goal in itself if peak-bagging isn't your thing. From here, views both north and south are spectacular. A small, dark pyramid of rock is the perfect place to sit and contemplate the mysterious energy of the ancient mountains that surround you.

If you're planning to score both peaks, start with Hiamovi Mountain. The "difficult" rating for these hikes comes from the robust elevation gain more than anything technical. Lining up bearings for the off-trail portions is reasonably simple. I'd highly recommend spending a few moments at Hiamovi Plateau, even if just to enjoy a snack.

GETTING THERE: These hikes share the Roaring Fork trailhead with Watanga Lake/Mountain (page 24). Follow US-34 north from the town of Granby. For Front Rangers, this means taking I-70 west to US-40 over Berthoud Pass and through the town of Winter Park. From the junction of US-40 and US-34, take US-34 for 5.4 miles and turn right onto CO-6. At the start of this road is a pay kiosk for the Arapaho National Rec-

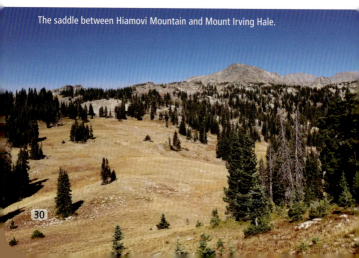

The saddle between Hiamovi Mountain and Mount Irving Hale.

A very special place in the IPW—Hiamovi Plateau.

reation Area ($5 for day use as of 2019). Follow this impressive dirt road 8.8 miles along the southwest shore of Lake Granby, then take a left onto CO 637 at the Big Rock Campground. Follow this road 0.8 mile farther to the Roaring Fork trailhead on your right. The trailhead is a roundabout with plenty of parking and is accessible to passenger cars. There is no additional fee to park here.

If coming from the Denver/Boulder metro area, this is a long drive—about 2 hours and 45 minutes. It may be worth reserving a site at one of the campgrounds in the area: Big Rock, Moraine, or Arapaho Bay. You can snag a site by visiting the Arapaho National Recreation Area (ANRA) website.

THE ROUTE: Begin at the Roaring Fork Trail and head up. You'll gain elevation right out of the gate, then level off to a more gradual grade until the intersection with the Watanga Lake Trail. At this intersection (2.4 miles), stay right on the Roaring Fork Trail. Get ready to work, the next 1.3 miles promises a stiff 1,430 feet of vertical gain, albeit on a well-maintained trail.

At a wide-open meadow, the Roaring Fork Trail reaches the saddle between Hiamovi Mountain and Mount Irving Hale. There is no signage here and the trail itself is a thin ribbon through the alpine grass. It's decision time! Hiamovi's hidden summit cannot be seen from here but awaits to the north and Irving Hale is to the south. If you decide to combine the two, Hiamovi is the tougher of the pair and is advised to do first.

From the saddle, your first objective is to get off trail and reach the Hiamovi Plateau. Navigate north through pine

Scrappy boulders on Hiamovi.   Summit cairn on Mount Irving Hale.

trees, rounded rock gardens, and short, punchy hills for 0.5 mile to reach the broad plateau. The boulder-riddled south ridge is now in plain view—if you like boulder hopping on semi-steady rock, go for it! This is the most direct line to the top. For better footing, skirt left around the shoulder of the ridge until you find a suitable line on the west slopes.

At around 12,200 feet (roughly 1.2 miles from the saddle), the terrain flattens out and the summit of Hiamovi comes into view to the northeast. Continue 0.2 mile to this craggy summit and count yourself among the few to visit this magical place. To return to the Roaring Fork Trail, find your way back to Hiamovi Plateau and be sure not to trend too far left. The saddle will be visually obvious most of the way back, making for an easy bearing.

The semi-clear-cut ramp south of the saddle is a pleasant prelude to the rocky summit area of Mount Irving Hale. There's something of a faint trail here, but don't worry if you lose it. The way up is straightforward. Climb the grassy ramp and pass through a field hitting the black boulders below the peak. Scramble to the summit in your own style from here. Stay left for more scrambling or to the right of the boulder field to circle around for more of a walk-up. There are a few easy moves up to the summit block, which has stunning views of Lake Granby and Hiamovi Mountain (among others), as well as some dramatic exposure just beyond the summit confines. Return down the way you came to the saddle and the Roaring Fork Trail.

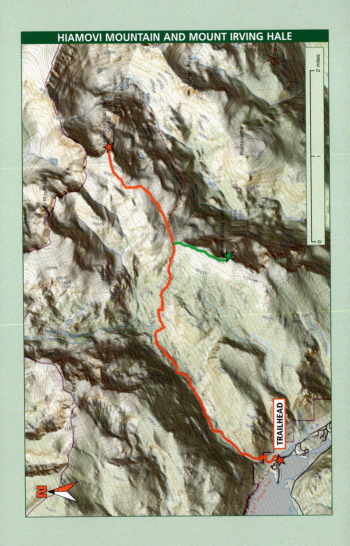

TRAILHEAD

4. Gourd Lake

RATING	Moderate
ROUND-TRIP DISTANCE	15 miles
ROUND-TRIP TIME	6–8 hours
ELEVATION GAIN	2,700 feet
MAP	Trails Illustrated #102, Indian Peaks, Gold Hill; Latitude 40° Maps - Boulder County, Front Range
NEAREST LANDMARK	Lake Granby

COMMENT: Gourd Lake (10,820 feet) gets my vote for the most beautiful lake in the Indian Peaks Wilderness. It's a wonderful place to camp overnight but it's also a great day hike. The long mileage is due in part to the fact that the trails to Gourd Lake are very backpacker friendly—long switchbacks keep the low terrain angle but add to the overall distance. . Never too steep, well maintained, and plenty of switchbacks make this a Class 1 affair. Gourd Lake sits in a spectacular amphitheater of white rock, where defiant stands of pine trees are watched over by the impressive citadel of 12,296-foot Cooper Peak. For the hiker who is laser-focused on

Gourd Lake, arguably the most beautiful lake in the IPW.

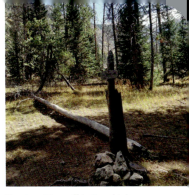

the ascent, the hike down from Gourd Lake offers spectacular views of 11,938-foot Thunderbolt Peak, 12,304-foot Sawtooth Mountain, and 13,088-foot Paiute Peak.

The signed turn-off to Gourd Lake.

The approach on the Cascade Creek Trail highlights the beauty of the wilderness on the western side of the Indian Peaks Wilderness. Expect the gentle flutter of aspen leaves, silos of sunlight illuminating the forest floor, and diamond flashes sparkling off the steadily flowing Cascade Creek. Moose and black bear are common sights, especially around Monarch Lake.

Thanks to the low elevation, this hike stays in trees, making it a fine option for days with a spotty weather forecast. It's possible to hike up to Buchanan Pass by staying on the Buchanan Pass Trail, 3.5 miles past the Gourd Lake turnoff, for an 8.7-mile one-way adventure (or a whopping 17.4-mile out-and-back). This option may appeal to trail runners or backpackers hoping to plan out a few days in the Buchanan Zone backcountry.

Thunderbolt Peak from the Gourd Lake Trail.

Dedicated peak baggers may be interested in bagging Marten Peak (12,041 feet) and Cooper Peak (12,296 feet) from Gourd Lake. Both are Class 3 scrambles that require good off-trail navigation to reach. Unless you have beast-mode level of fitness, doing this in a day isn't a great option. Camping at Gourd Lake and taking on the summits the next day is the way to go—you'll also score a glimpse at the even-higher Island Lake at 11,420 feet, the sister lake to Gourd Lake.

As a final note, the Cascade Creek Trail goes 6.2 miles past the junction with the Buchanan Pass Trail all the way to the top of Pawnee Pass. The Crater Lake Trail is off Cascade Creek and is a very popular camping destination, thanks to the incredible view of Lone Eagle Peak from Mirror Lake.

GETTING THERE: The Monarch Lake trailhead is the main gateway to the western IPW. Don't be surprised if the parking lot is full on summer weekends (parking is allowed along the road except where signed). Crowds tend to disperse among the many trails that start here, with the majority heading to Crater Lake. To get there, follow US-34 north from the town of Granby. For Front Rangers, this means taking I-70 west to US-40 over Berthoud Pass and through the town of Winter Park. From the junction of US-40 and Highway 34, take US-34 for 5.4 miles, then take a right turn onto CO-6. At the start of this road is a pay kiosk for the Arapaho National Recreation Area ($5 for day use as of 2019). Follow the dirt road 9.8 miles along the southwestern shore of Lake Granby, past the Big Rock Campground, to the end of the road and parking area. There is a gate, ranger station, kiosk, and plenty of signage at the start of the lake trails.

THE BEST INDIAN PEAKS WILDERNESS HIKES

THE ROUTE: Pass the gate at the east side of the parking lot and begin your day on the Cascade Creek Trail. Unlike many Colorado mountain hikes, this one gives you nearly 1.0 mile of flat to warm up your legs. Enjoy scenery along the north shore of Monarch Lake, where the moose roam free. After 1.5 miles, stay on the Cascade Creek Trail at the junction with the Arapaho Pass Trail. Continue another 1.7 miles and take a left onto the Buchanan Pass Trail.

On some maps (both digital and paper), the Gourd Lake Trail is shown at a spot where the Buchanan Pass Trail crosses a small creek. This is NOT the case. The Gourd Lake Trail is signed and is very much an established trail. Make sure to pass the stony creek bed (which may or may not be running) and continue on farther to the correct trail turnoff. The actual turnoff for the Gourd Lake Trail is at 5.2 miles, just before a large clearing with lots of windblown trees. Take a left and begin the climb up to the lake along a well-made trail featuring several accommodating switchbacks.

A small pond at 7.4 miles serves as the opening act for Gourd Lake. Pass it and follow the social trails around the lake at your leisure. The first part of Gourd Lake that you'll see is the "stem" of the lake. Cooper Peak offers a photogenic background here, but keep walking around to see the full scope of the lake. Waterfalls roll down from the north slopes and the lake is revealed to be quite large. Relax, enjoy, and return at your leisure.

Cooper Peak from Gourd Lake.

5. Crater Lake

RATING	Moderate
ROUND-TRIP DISTANCE	14 miles
ROUND-TRIP TIME	7–9 hours
ELEVATION GAIN	2,500 feet
MAP	Trails Illustrated #102, Indian Peaks, Gold Hill; Latitude 40° Maps - Boulder County, Front Range
NEAREST LANDMARK	Monarch Lake

COMMENT: Crater Lake (10,315 feet) is more popular as an overnight backpacking destination than as a day hike, thanks to a long 14-mile route out-and-back. For strong hikers and trail runners, however, a full day out means Crater Lake can be done as a single outing. Day hikers have several things in their favor: the trails in are excellent and gain elevation gradually, plus they are all below treeline so storms are less dangerous than other destinations. Despite the long mileage, it's easy to move quickly on the well-maintained trails to this memorable locale. That being said, camping at

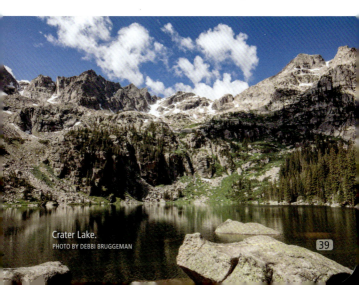

Crater Lake.
PHOTO BY DEBBI BRUGGEMAN

Crater Lake is a wonderful experience and is a great way to enjoy a weekend (permits are required from June—September, see page 19 for details).

Many photographers come to shoot Lone Eagle Peak from Crater Lake's runoff pool, called Mirror Lake. It is perhaps the single most iconic shot in the Indian Peaks Wilderness.

The Cascade Trail goes another 3.2 miles past the turnoff for Crater Lake, ending at Pawnee Pass. It is possible to reach Crater Lake from the Long Lake trailhead (page 57), but it's roughly 8.5 miles one-way—a 17-mile out-and-back with significant elevation gain. This option works better as a backpacking strategy, although your author has done this route as a long day hike.

Lone Eagle Peak has the most exhilarating standard route of any Indian Peak summit but falls outside the scope of this guide due to its technical Class 4–5 ridge with dizzying exposure. Lone Eagle Peak's standard route, *Solo Flight,* is covered in Dave Cooper's excellent guide *Colorado Scrambles* (CMC Press) and on many online websites.

GETTING THERE: The Monarch Lake trailhead is the main gateway to the western IPW. Don't be surprised if the parking lot is full on summer weekends (parking is allowed along the road except where signed). Crowds tend to disperse among the many trails that start here, with the majority heading to Crater Lake. To get there, follow US-34 north from the town of Granby. For Front Rangers, this means taking I-70 west to

Monarch Lake.

A blazing sunrise from Mirror Lake. Lone Eagle Peak's imposing summit spire dominates the skyline. PHOTO BY BART DEFERME

US-40 over Berthoud Pass and through the town of Winter Park. From the junction of US-40 and US-34, take US-34 for 5.4 miles, then take a right turn onto CO-6. At the start of this road is a pay kiosk for the Arapaho National Recreation Area ($5 for day use as of 2019). Follow the dirt road 9.8 miles along the southwestern shore of Lake Granby, past the Big Rock Campground, to the end of the road and parking area. There is a gate, ranger station, kiosk, and plenty of signage at the start of the lake trails.

THE ROUTE: The easy, flat start of this adventure begins on the Cascade Creek Trail on the northeastern shores of Monarch Lake. After 1.5 miles, stay on the Cascade Creek Trail at a junction with the Arapaho Pass Trail. The forest section here is gorgeous, even by Colorado's high standards.

Stay on the Cascade Creek Trail at the junction with Buchanan Pass (3.2 miles). From here, you'll be on the Cascade Creek Trail for 3.0 more miles. Turn right onto the signed Crater Lake Trail. Mirror Lake comes first, along with that classic view of Lone Eagle Peak. It's 0.1 mile from here to Crater Lake itself. It's possible to see both the Fair Glacier and Peck Glacier from the lake. Enjoy and return the way you came.

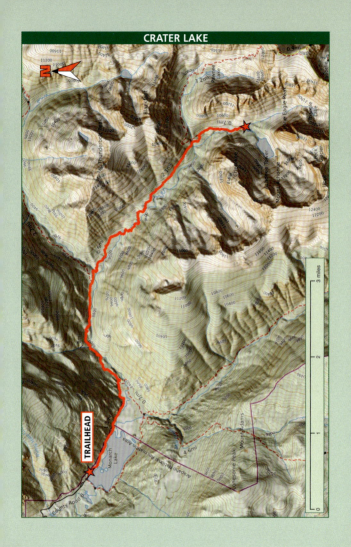

6. Mount Neva and Mount Jasper

RATING	Moderate to Difficult
ROUND-TRIP DISTANCE	10.2 miles out-and-back
ROUND-TRIP TIME	7–9 hours
ELEVATION GAIN	3,650 feet (both peaks)
MAP	Trails Illustrated #102, Indian Peaks, Gold Hill; Latitude 40° Maps - Boulder County, Front Range
NEAREST LANDMARK	Meadow Creek Reservoir
BOUNUS ROUTES	Mount Neva North Ridge - Mount Jasper East Ridge

COMMENT: Because there are no standard routes on Mount Neva (12,814 feet) and Mount Jasper (12,923 feet, also called Jasper Peak), there are a lot of options! And that doesn't take into consideration several classic snow routes. The route here (red line) approaches from the west via Columbine Lake and is the easiest way to tag both mountains.

The bonus routes are more challenging and approach from the east via the Fourth of July trailhead. It's also possible to

Mount Neva's exciting north ridge. PHOTO BY JAYME MOYE

Mount Neva's North Ridge. PHOTOS BY JAYME MOYE

access the northwest slopes for Mount Neva from the east by hiking over Arapaho and Caribou Passes, though this makes for a very long day hike. Camping at Columbine Lake is always an option to break up the adventure into two days.

The bonus routes both require confident navigational skills. The Class 2+ route via Jasper's northeast slopes presents no major technical hurdles but involves a challenging mile-long off-trail hike through a semi-forested basin. The Class 4 north ridge of Mount Neva requires good ridge-route finding and has some wild exposure, albeit on excellent rock—it is the most difficult route covered in this guide. The 1.2-mile hike between the peaks is my favorite traverse in the Indian Peaks (it's on the cover of this book).

The western approach from 4th of July trailhead showing Mount Jasper (left) and Mount Neva (right).

"Proper Summit of the Rocky Mountains" survey marker.

Keep your eyes peeled midway through the traverse between the peaks for a glass jar with a logbook and a brass USGS survey pin. The pin is located at the 40th latitude parallel, the most important survey point for plotting land in the mountain west. It was originally marked in 1859 by a survey team and later deemed the "Proper Summit of the Rocky Mountains" in 1867 by George Hill of the Hayden Survey. From this parallel, the land of the Kansas, Nebraska, and Colorado territories was eventually defined. A much more familiar incarnation of the 40th parallel is Boulder's Baseline Road.

GETTING THERE: The Junco Lake trailhead is reached from Tabernash on the west side of the IPW. From US-40 turn east onto County Road 84/FSR 129 for 11.0 miles along a beat-up, rutted road. Passenger cars aren't ideal but carefully driven, can make the trailhead. SUVs and sport-utility cars (Subaru Outback, Honda CRV) will be fine. The signed parking area for Junco Lake trailhead is south past the Meadow Creek Reservoir.

THE ROUTE: The easy part of the day involves hiking 3.1 miles on-trail to Columbine Lake. Start on the Caribou Pass Trail at the Junco Lake trailhead and enjoy a pleasant walk beside Meadow Creek. A few old cabins are tucked into the forest along the way.

At 1.8 miles, leave the Caribou Pass Trail and go right (south) on the Columbine Lake Trail. Elevation gain begins in earnest here. After another 1.3 miles, reach Columbine Lake where you'll see the fearsome north ridge of Mount Neva as well as the obvious break where the humble northwest slopes begin. Go off trail due south to an obvious saddle at 11,500 feet, where you will gain the slopes.

From Columbine Lake, it's about 1.2 miles (depending on your off-trail route) and 1,810 vertical feet to the summit of Mount Neva (12,814 feet). Faint trails may guide you, but don't count on them; visual navigation is easy. From here the taller Mount Jasper looms to the southeast. If you're in it for Mount Neva alone, return the way you came.

The traverse to Mount Jasper is 1.2 miles one-way along fun, Class 2+ scrambling. Descend off Mount Neva and begin the fantastic trek over to Mount Jasper. From the survey pin, continue along the curling ridge to the pristine peak of Mount Jasper, which offers great views west to Winter Park and the Gore Range and east to the foothills and plains. On the return back to Columbine Lake, there's no reason to revisit the summit of Mount Neva. Stay west on the slopes and aim for the saddle that will bring you back to Columbine Lake and the trails home.

Mount Jasper East Ridge: While only Class 2, the challenge for this route (yellow line) is 0.5-mile of off-trail navigation in a semi-dense forest. I happen to love this kind of navigation, but it requires skill with a map and compass—a good GPS device makes things easier. Plan on 8 to 10 hours of hiking. From the Fourth of July trailhead (page 85), take the Arapaho Pass Trail 1.0 mile to the Diamond Lake Trail. Take the Diamond Lake Trail for 0.4 mile. When it crosses Middle Boulder Creek, get off-trail and navigate the drainage southwest through spongy woods up loose, rocky hills to treeline. Once you reach a pair of lakes at 11,775 feet, navigation is much easier. There is a small plane wreck at the eastern lake (known informally as Lake Xanadu). Chug up the slopes to connect with Jasper's northeast ridge. If there is still snow (usually through June) you'll want crampons here. At 3.5 miles, reach the summit of Mount Jasper. From here you can hike north to Neva in 1.2 miles. The easiest way to return is to descend north to the saddle between Neva, then drop into a basin north of where you ascended (purple line), where the off-trail navigation is almost all above treeline back to Arapaho Pass Trail.

Mount Neva North Ridge: This incredible, thrilling Class 4 route (green line) is mentioned in light detail because it is

Columbine Lake.

reserved for experienced climbers with strong route-finding skills that can handle prolonged sections of high exposure. But wow, is it fun for those who love a good scramble! Allow 7 to 9 hours for this adventure. From the Fourth of July Trailhead (page 85), hike 2.5 miles to Lake Dorothy and get off-trail to gain the obvious ridge. The ridge is 0.9 mile to the summit. The lion's share of the scrambling is Class 3 on excellent rock. Much of the route's best terrain stays left (east) of the ridge on ledges and rock ramps. The crux is an intimidating notch at around 12,600 feet that is a 30-foot scramble. If the fall potential wasn't so high here, it would be considered a Class 3+ section. Handholds and footholds are abundant and confident climbers will have no problem getting past it. What follows is a section of exposed Class 3 terrain that finally yields to the northwest slopes shortly before the summit.

Even for experienced climbers, it's not advised to return via the north ridge. The easiest way back is via the saddle between Neva and Jasper (purple line). The least steep slopes are closer to Jasper on its north face. If there is snow, crampons may be needed to descend the top part of this slope. If you're uncertain, it's always possible to return via the northwest slopes of Neva to Columbine Lake and slog back over Caribou and Arapaho Passes.

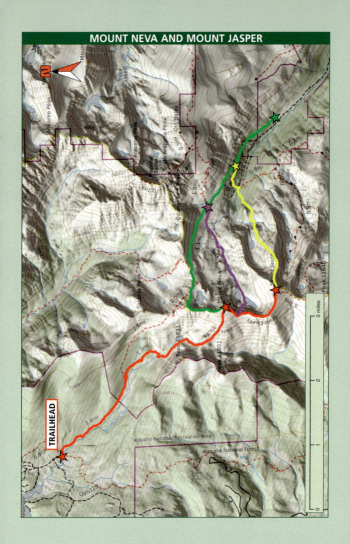

TRAILHEAD

7. Sawtooth Mountain

RATING	Moderate
ROUND-TRIP DISTANCE	14.1 miles from Beaver Reservoir trailhead (7.3 miles from Coney Flats trailhead 4x4 parking)
ROUND-TRIP TIME	7–10 hours
ELEVATION GAIN	3,300 feet
MAP	Trails Illustrated #102, Indian Peaks, Gold Hill; Latitude 40° Maps - Boulder County, Front Range
NEAREST LANDMARK	Ward
BONUS	Red Deer Lake - Red Deer Mountain

COMMENT: Sawtooth Mountain's distinct shark fin shape cuts an impressive profile when viewed from the east, especially at sunset. Don't let the long mileage discourage you from visiting this magnificent peak—the hike goes quicker than the distance implies. The approach is a mellow 3.3 miles on shaded 4x4 roads to Coney Flats trailhead. After that, the route to the summit passes through a surprisingly lush forest featuring a dramatic breakthrough above treeline. The final ascent up Buchanan Pass follows a Class 1 trail to a saddle between Sawtooth Mountain and neighboring Red Deer

Western section of the Buchanan Pass Trail.

Entry point of the Beaver Creek Trail.

Lush alpine growth along the Beaver Creek Trail.

Mountain. While there are no formal trails to the top, the accommodating summit slopes make for easy hill walking.

Besides Sawtooth Mountain (12,304 feet), there are some quality options in the area. Below treeline, Red Deer Lake (10,377 feet) is a fine destination in its own right. Red Deer Mountain (12,391 feet) stands to the north of Sawtooth Mountain above the Buchanan Pass saddle, which the two peaks share. It's a straightforward walk-up that can be extended out to Peak 12,277 via a broad ridge. Note that Sawtooth Mountain can also be reached by the western approach via Buchanan Pass (see page 34 "Gourd Lake" for details on this route).

GETTING THERE: The standard trailhead is located on the north shore of Beaver Reservoir and is accessible by passenger cars. From the south, take CO-72 (Peak-to-Peak Highway) 2.6 miles past the intersection with Brainard Lake Road in Ward and turn left onto Beaver Reservoir Road. As of 2018, there is a "Boy Scout Camp" sign at this turn.

From the north, the right turn onto Beaver Reservoir Road from CO-72 is 7.6 miles past the intersection of CO-72 and CO-7.

Follow this dirt road 2.5 miles to the informal but established Beaver Reservoir trailhead. Parking is a few hundred feet past a cement overflow dip and begins at a well-signed 4x4 road—a closure gate may or may not be open. Do not park in front of the gate. If the few parking spots are full, park along the road on the right-hand side.

NOTE: From the Beaver Reservoir trailhead, it's possible to reach the Coney Flats parking area via the Coney Flats 4x4 road, but it is *not recommended* for stock SUVs. You will need a serious Jeep, ATV, or similar dedicated off-road vehicle. There are several burly rock obstacles along the way and a deep, permanent pool of water just before the parking area.

THE ROUTE: Hike west through the well-signed gate and follow the 4x4 road, Coney Flats Road. Thankfully, it feels more like a double-track trail than a dirt road. It is well-shaded and it's easy to move briskly. There are a few side paths off the main road to the left along the way, but stay the course on the obvious primary road. After 1.5 miles, a marked hiker's trail goes straight off Coney Flats Road, which veers uphill to the left. Go straight on the hikers' trail, which is closed to motorized traffic. Enjoy the solitude for 1.2 miles, when this footpath rejoins Coney Flats Road. Continue straight a short distance to the Coney Flats trailhead. A low-budget, narrow-but-sturdy footbridge skirts the large pool to the far side of the trailhead.

At 3.3 miles, the Coney Flats trailhead is a large, open area with fantastic views of Sawtooth Mountain. This is the end of the 4x4 road terrain. The Beaver Creek Trail begins at a prominent wood "Indian Peaks Wilderness" sign on the far

Sawtooth's surprisingly rounded summit.

west side of the trailhead. Head west on the Beaver Creek Trail for 0.3 mile toward Buchanan Pass. Pass a junction for the Coney Lake Trail on your left. Stay straight on the Beaver Creek Trail. This section of the trail goes through beautiful and dense foliage and over a few small creeks as it gradually ascends. Moose are a common sight here.

In 1.3 miles, the Beaver Creek Trail ends as the Buchanan Pass Trail merges in from the right (north) and takes over. Stay straight (west) on the newly designated Buchanan Pass Trail toward the high saddle in the distance. This trail segment up to the pass is one the most enjoyable in the Indian Peaks. It has a mellow grade as it climbs 1.3 miles into the alpine tundra and the foot of Sawtooth Mountain.

Just before the final push to Buchanan Pass, the trail splits into a direct line and a wide switchback. Both are established, worn-in trails and connect to the same spot. The switchback trail to the right (north) is the actual trail. Pick your path and carry on to the top of the pass, which offers incredible views of the deep, mysterious western side of the Indian Peaks Wilderness.

Sawtooth's summit slopes are waiting to your left (south) and offer an easy, off-trail walk-up. Pushy winds are common. The wide-open, broad summit of Sawtooth Mountain is mercifully not razor-thin. To the south, the ridge connecting Mount Audubon and Paiute Peak (page 62) looks intense, as does the craggy, broken northeast face of Paiute Peak. The interesting hill just southeast of Sawtooth Mountain is

Sawtooth's summit slopes are actually quite tame.

Sawtooth's summit fin can be admired from as far away as Boulder.

11,565-foot "Coney Island," an unofficially named summit. Enjoy these majestic views and return the way you came.

Red Deer Mountain and Peak 12,277: Peakbaggers will be rightfully tempted to walk up neighboring Red Deer Mountain off Buchanan Pass. It's roughly a 0.5-mile off-trail via the south slopes to the top, which is 87 feet higher than the summit of Sawtooth. From Red Deer, it's 0.8 mile farther along a northwest, Class 2 ridge to Point 12,277, a rarely visited but worthy summit that offers views of the St. Vrain glaciers and the peaks of Rocky Mountain National Park to the north.

Red Deer Lake: This is a great detour—or a way to salvage the day if storms are moving in before you're close to Buchanan Pass. At the western terminus of the Beaver Creek Trail, the Buchanan Pass Trail heads downhill to the north. Follow it 0.8 mile to gain the left (west) turnoff for the Red Deer Lake Trail. In 2019, this "sign" was a blank post with "Red Deer Lake" hand carved into it (hopefully this will be replaced soon). Follow the Red Deer Lake Trail uphill 0.5 mile to this gorgeous alpine lake.

8. Pawnee Pass Area

RATING	Moderate
ROUND-TRIP DISTANCE	8.8 miles Pawnee Pass; 9.6 miles Shoshoni Peak; 9.6 miles Pawnee Peak; 10.8 miles Mount Toll
ROUND-TRIP TIME	5–7 hours Pawnee Pass; 5–7 hours Shoshoni Peak; 5–7 hours Pawnee Peak; 6–8 hours Mount Toll
ELEVATION GAIN	2,140 feet Pawnee Pass; 2,615 feet Shoshoni Peak; 2,525 feet Pawnee Peak; 3,300 feet Mount Toll
MAP	Trails Illustrated #102, Indian Peaks, Gold Hill; Latitude 40° Maps - Boulder County, Front Range
NEAREST LANDMARK	Ward

COMMENT: Pawnee Pass (12,550 feet) is the gateway to three excellent IPW summits and is a wonderful destination in its own right. Even though there is a lot of information stuffed into this chapter, it could have been even more extensive. As it is, Long Lake and Lake Isabelle are en route, as well as great views of Isabelle Glacier, the Navajo snowfield, and Navajo Peak. On top of all that, the Pawnee Pass Trail ends where the Cascade Creek Trail begins, opening up a large swath of

Lots of work went into crafting the Pawnee Pass Trail.

the western IPW, including Pawnee Lake, Crater Lake, the ominous needle of Lone Eagle Peak, and much more.

Pawnee Peak (12,943 feet) and Mount Toll (12,979 feet) are easy walk-up summits from Pawnee Pass. This route is the least difficult way to access Mount Toll, considered by some to be the centerpiece of the Indian Peaks Wilderness. Head the opposite way off the pass and you're on your way to Shoshoni Peak (12,967 feet). Shoshoni's "crow's nest" summit turret is one of the most unique mountaintops in Colorado and it always puts a goofy smile on my face to stand in the nest.

For a more casual day, you could simply ignore Pawnee Pass and stay on the Lake Isabelle Trail, which terminates at the start of the Isabelle Glacier. Even though Pawnee Pass is a popular trail, it's also a good workout. Many backpackers who stay at Pawnee Lake or Crater Lake prefer to go up and over Pawnee Pass versus entering from the Monarch Lake trailhead.

The combo of Pawnee and Toll is a special hike because it offers views of every facet of the IPW: the jagged, defiant ridges of the west, the forested peaks to the north, the glaciated lakes and creeks to the east, and the strange combination of all these forces in the distinct mountains to the south.

Lake Isabelle at sunrise.

Shoshoni Peak's summit block from the Pawnee Pass Trail.

GETTING THERE: Pawnee Pass starts from the Long Lake trail-head at the Brainard Lake Recreation Area (which is also the jumping off point to two other hikes in this guide). The turnoff to Brainard Lake Road is off CO-72 (Peak-to-Peak Highway) in Ward. From Nederland, this is 11.8 miles from the roundabout onto CO-72. It's also possible to get here by driving up Left Hand Canyon, through Ward, and turning right onto CO-72. The left (west) turn onto the well-marked Brainard Lake Road is about 200 feet past the junction of CO-72 and the top of Left Hand Canyon Drive (called Nelson Road on some maps).

Brainard Lake Road was repaved and improved in 2018, making for a smooth ride. It's 2.5 miles to the toll gate/ winter parking lot, then another 2.5 miles to the Long Lake trailhead. Note this access road was recently re-routed south along Brainard Lake. Follow the road around the lake to the west side, then take a left onto the well-marked road to the trailhead.

As of 2019, it is $11 per vehicle / $6 for motorcycle / $1 for pedestrians and cyclists for a 3-day pass. The America the Beautiful Pass and the American Land & Leisure Pass are both accepted as well. Once the gate closes (usually around mid-October), there are no fees and you'll have to park in the winter lot.

A word of warning: all of the Brainard Lake parking lots fill up very early on summer/autumn weekends. I've seen packed lots at 5:30 am—assume they are full by 6:00 am. If you're late, you'll either have to wait until a spot opens (which can literally take hours) or park in the winter lot and hike or bike in. Alternative strategies include hiking mid-week or reserving a camp spot at Pawnee Campground.

THE ROUTE: From the Long Lake trailhead, take the Long Lake Trail to … you guessed it … Long Lake! Stay on this trail as it passes two junctions with the Jean Lunning Trail, which simply circles around the other side of Long Lake. After 1.7 miles, start gaining elevation as you cross the flower-festooned waterfall just before reaching Lake Isabelle.

At Lake Isabelle, turn off the trail right (north) on the signed Pawnee Pass Trail. From here, the trail steadily climbs up switchbacks, along ledges, and above treeline. As the trail gets steeper, views open up to the south and the east. The shimmering water of the lakes below is photographic gold in the early morning light.

The trail section from Lake Isabelle to the wide-open slopes of Pawnee Pass is a trail building masterpiece. The quality of this route is exceptional and IPW work crews donate their time every year to keep this heavily used trail in excellent shape. Continue 2.6 miles upward until reaching the elegant saddle plateau of Pawnee Pass, where strong winds are com-

Nearing the top of Pawnee Pass.

Looking back at the descent gully off Shoshoni Peak.

mon. Many times, the wind on summits and ridges is less intense than in the saddle. The highest point of Pawnee Pass is a memorable destination. If this is your goal for the day, it's worth walking over to the west a few hundred feet to catch a glimpse of the western IPW. Head back the way you came when it's time to go, for an 8.8-mile out-and-back day.

Pawnee Peak: From Pawnee Pass, it's 0.4 mile and 385 vertical feet up the grassy south slopes to this domed summit. For those who want just a little bit more out of their day up Pawnee Pass, this is a fine option. It's also possible to continue north from Pawnee Peak to Mount Toll.

Hiking just Pawnee Peak adds 0.8 mile to your total day, for a 9.6-mile out-and-back.

Mount Toll: Mount Toll offers the same open, hilly terrain as Pawnee Peak. It's 0.6 mile from Pawnee Peak to Mount Toll, with 380 feet of elevation gain. From Pawnee Pass, it's a 2.0-mile out-and-back to Mount Toll, with a total of 1,190 feet of elevation gain, thanks to having to descend the saddle between Pawnee Peak and Mount Toll and regain it on the way back. Adding Toll into your day makes for a hearty 10.8-mile out-and-back day with 3,300 feet of elevation gain total.

The thrilling final ramp to Shoshoni's summit.

Shoshoni Peak: The hike to Shoshoni involves some light scrambling but is otherwise straightforward. It's a more robust adventure than Pawnee/Toll. To begin, head south from Pawnee Pass and skirt east of Peak 12,878 (which, for all intents, looks like a "real" peak from this perspective). Continue over a boulder field to a pleasant patch of alpine tundra. Shoshoni's distinct tilted chimney summit is a beacon in the distance. When you reach the summit tower (1.0 mile from Pawnee Pass and 475 feet of vertical gain), you'll have to perform a brave scrambling move to get into the crow's nest—it's a little bit exposed, but on good rock with solid holds all around.

To return, you could simply walk back to Pawnee Pass, which is a bit tedious. To save time, head east off the summit and traverse out to where this ridge nears an end. From here, head down the northeast slopes via a gully, grassy slopes, and a few loose rock sections. Note that closer to the summit, the slopes tend to cliff out, so staying farther east will offer the better footing. Reach a small shelf of pools and tall grass before reconnecting with the Pawnee Pass Trail, about 1.4 miles from your start at Pawnee Pass. This option is about 9.6 miles with 2,615 feet of elevation gain.

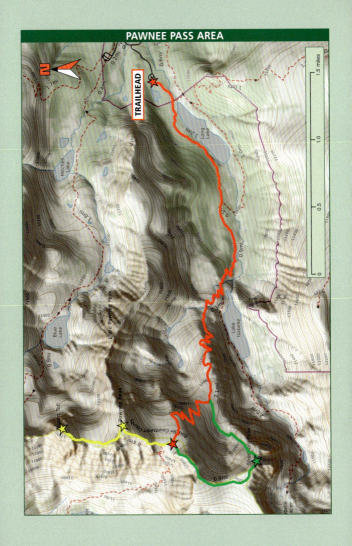

TRAILHEAD

1.5 miles

1.0

0.5

0

THE BEST INDIAN PEAKS WILDERNESS HIKES

9. Mount Audubon and Paiute Peak

RATING	Mount Audubon, Moderate; Pauite Traverse, Difficult
ROUND-TRIP DISTANCE	7.7 miles Mount Audubon; 9.5 miles Paiute Peak via Mount Audubon; 8.2 miles Paiute Peak via Blue Lake
ROUND-TRIP TIME	5–7 hours Mount Audubon; 7–9 hours Paiute Peak
ELEVATION GAIN	2,700 feet Mount Audubon; 3,300 feet Paiute Peak
MAP	Trails Illustrated #102, Indian Peaks, Gold Hill; Latitude 40° Maps - Boulder County, Front Range
NEAREST LANDMARK	Ward

COMMENT: Mount Audubon (13,223 feet) is *the* classic Indian Peaks summit hike. Its familiar dome dominates the skyline from the east, especially from the high mesas near Boulder. Those looking for their first IPW summit will feel rightly accomplished atop the fourth highest mountain in the Wilderness. For many locals, Audubon is an old friend. The traverse over to Paiute Peak (13,088 feet) adds an exciting extension to the day. This superb Class 3 traverse demands respect. Finding the best scrambling lines can be challenging near the summit and there are a few brief moments of exposure. If you're okay with a little talus scrambling, it's possible to make a loop off Paiute by scrambling down to Blue Lake, where the Blue Lake Trail will guide you home.

The saddle between Mount Audubon and the cheekily named "Mount Notabon" is famous for delivering fierce winds. This is why the high slopes of the mountain are seldom snowy, even in the dead of winter. From this blustery point, Audubon's established trail fades away and a short but exciting scramble heads to the summit. For many hikers,

Mount Audubon (right) from Brainard Lake.

this sequence—and the resulting sense of accomplishment—unlocks a love for mountain adventures in the Indian Peaks.

Many people summit Audubon alone before coming back and tackling the Paiute Peak traverse. As mentioned above, it's a long, tough day and there have been accidents on this traverse due to weather moving in and poor navigation along the ridge. But for confident, fit hikers, it's easy to keep the route at Class 3 and it's one of the most thrilling traverses in the IPW.

If you want a double summit day without the scrambling, little ol' 12,711-foot Mount Notabon is a fun add-on. After tagging Audubon, return to the saddle and wander off-trail to the summit of this scrappy pile of rock. Notabon has a boulder field on its summit skirt but the rock is mostly solid and the footing is good Class 2 terrain. Trend back to the Mount Audubon Trail off of Notabon. The detour will add less than 1.0 mile to your overall day.

GETTING THERE: The Mount Audubon Trail starts at the popular Mitchell Lake trailhead located within the Brainard Lake Recreation Area. The turnoff to Brainard Lake Road is off CO-72 (Peak-to-Peak Highway) in Ward. From Nederland, this is 11.8 miles from the roundabout turn onto CO-72. It's also possible to get here by driving up Left Hand Canyon, through Ward, and turning right onto CO-72. The left (west) turn to the well-marked Brainard Lake Road is about 200 feet past the junction of CO-72 and the top of Left Hand Canyon Drive (called Nelson Road on some maps).

Brainard Lake Road was repaved and improved in 2018, making for a smooth ride. It's 2.5 miles to the toll gate/winter parking lot, then another 2.8 miles to the Mitchell Lake trailhead. Note this access road was re-routed south along Brainard Lake. Follow it to the parking lot at the end of the road.

As of 2019, it is $11 per vehicle / $6 for motorcycle / $1 for pedestrians and cyclists for a 3-day pass. The America the Beautiful Pass and the American Land & Leisure Pass are both accepted as well. Once the gate closes (usually around mid-October), there are no fees and you'll have to park in the winter lot.

A word of warning: all of the Brainard Lake parking lots fill up very early on summer/autumn weekends. I've seen packed lots at 5:30 am—assume they are full by 6:00 am. If you're late, you'll either have to wait until a spot opens (which can literally take hours) or park in the winter lot and hike or bike in. Alternative strategies include hiking mid-week or reserving a camp spot at Pawnee Campground.

THE ROUTE: Start at the marked trailhead for the Mount Audubon Trail. Take the Mount Audubon/Beaver Creek Trail as it gradually makes its way through the vanilla-scented pine for-

North of Mount Audubon is the rocky, rounded hill known as Coney Island.

Alpine flowers on Audubon's south slopes.

The rocky transistion out of treeline.

est. The lower grade terrain lasts about 1.0 mile. After that, it begins climbing up a series of switchbacks as it ascends to the upper reaches of timberline. As you gain Audubon's east slopes and break out of treeline, the trail becomes peppered with small, loose rocks. The trail is easy to follow, but the footing requires a bit of extra attention.

As views expand and open up, the Mount Audubon Trail splits from the Beaver Creek at 1.7 miles and heads east. Continue up along the rocky trail, eventually passing a marshy section with small pools of clear water. As you near the saddle, the winds may get very strong. Interestingly, the winds in the saddle are often stronger than on the summit!

After 3.4 miles, the formal trail ends at 12,690 feet at the saddle. From here, a network of improvised trails scramble up the north face of Mount Audubon. The terrain is Class 2 and you may need to dab a hand down in spots. There's no one "right" trail, though as a rule, you'll want to stay left (east) for the most efficient line up. At 13,200 feet, the broad summit area opens up. It's a short walk to the top from here. There are several sturdy wind shelters to take respite from gusts. If Audubon was your goal, return the way you came for a 7.7-mile round trip, give or take the mileage, depending on how directly you scrambled to the summit.

If your desire is to continue to Paiute Peak, fuel up your body and get ready to scramble! As a word of warning, if the

Views from a winter ascent of Mount Audubon.

winds are strong, this can be a sketchy traverse. The ridge is direct, dead-west, with fun Class 3 scrambling along mostly solid rock. There is a bit of exposure near the summit of Paiute Peak but the rock is good. It's 0.9 mile between the two summits.

From here, you can see into all four directional realms of the Indian Peaks Wilderness. To return, you can either retrace your scramble back up to Audubon (ugh, 9.5 miles round trip) or descend talus slopes by scrambling south off Paiute on Class 3 rock, then dropping down before the saddle between Paiute and a small bump on the ridge between Paiute and Mount Toll. These loose but manageable slopes head down to Blue Lake, where the popular Blue Lake Trail will lead you back to the parking lot. This is a spectacular basin and is worth the visit.

My two cents: If you have the fitness and confidence to make the traverse to Paiute, then closing the loop by descending to Blue Lake will be no problem. It is much more fun than returning back over Mount Audubon. The visual off-trail navigation to Blue Lake is easy. That said, it is a long and physically taxing day. The trip to Paiute isn't for beginners or casual hikers.

When you reach the Blue Lake/Mitchell Lake Trail (and likely, crowds of hikers), follow it back to the trailhead.

10. Little Pawnee Peak

RATING	Difficult
ROUND-TRIP DISTANCE	5.8 miles
ROUND-TRIP TIME	5–6 hours
ELEVATION GAIN	1,910 feet
MAP	Trails Illustrated #102, Indian Peaks, Gold Hill; Latitude 40° Maps - Boulder County, Front Range
NEAREST LANDMARK	Ward

COMMENT: Little Pawnee Peak's benign moniker makes it seem like an alpine afterthought—at best, an insignificant summit with an adorable name. The truth is this gutsy 12,466-foot peak packs a lot of thrill into a daring half-day. Even though it's accessed from Brainard Lake's most popular trailhead, Long Lake, don't expect to see many other people after hopping off-trail. It is an open secret and yet, even scrambling junkies tend to miss it.

Before reaching the nitty-gritty terrain, a relatively easy-to-navigate off-trail segment ascends through an open forest, eventually breaking treeline on Little Pawnee's east ridge. Unique views of familiar peaks are one of the many treats

Approaching the scrambling.

Little Pawnee Peak packs a lot of action into a relatively short day.

this scramble offers. In the last 0.5 mile, the ridge narrows as the solid rock transforms into fun, Class 3 scrambling with some significant exposure. The crux lies just before the summit—a 25-foot downclimb into a narrow, off-camber gully. I err on the side of caution in calling this crux a Class 4 move, though depending on your height, you may find it to be easier (read the route description for details). A short rope to protect this section is a fine idea, as are helmets. By the time you reach the summit, any notion of Little Pawnee Peak lacking adventure will be gone.

For the experienced and the daring, it's possible to traverse to Pawnee Peak from Little Pawnee Peak. It's a legit Class 4 (or even low Class 5) route with difficult route finding, rotten rock, and deceptive passages. It's also a lot of fun—but beyond the scope of this guide, given its technical nature. Dave Cooper's *Colorado Scrambles* (CMC Press) has great details for this route if you want to give it a go.

The crux notch on Little Pawnee's ridge seems to have deteriorated a bit over the years. This is due in part to the fact that certain footholds are little more than grassy patches with slanted rock underneath. Unlike many other similar ridge notches in the IPW, this one has no easy workaround. The notch itself is the easiest way down. Take your time and check hand and foot holds!

Most of the off-trail terrain is easy to navigate.

GETTING THERE: Little Pawnee Peak starts from the Long Lake trailhead at the Brainard Lake Recreation Area (which is also the jumping off point to two other hikes in this guide). The turnoff to Brainard Lake Road is off CO-72 (Peak-to-Peak Highway) in Ward. From Nederland, this is 11.8 miles from the roundabout onto CO-72. It's also possible to get here by driving up Left Hand Canyon, through Ward, and turning right onto CO-72. The left (west) turn to the well-marked Brainard Lake Road is about 200 feet past the junction of CO-72 and the top of Left Hand Canyon Drive (called Nelson Road on some maps).

Brainard Lake Road was repaved and improved in 2018, making for a smooth ride. It's 2.5 miles to the toll gate/winter parking lot, then another 2.5 miles to the Long Lake trailhead. Note this access road was recently re-routed south along Brainard Lake. Follow the road around the lake to the west side, then take a left onto the well-marked road to the trailhead.

As of 2019, it is $11 per vehicle / $6 for motorcycle / $1 for pedestrians and cyclists for a 3-day pass. The America the Beautiful Pass and the American Land & Leisure Pass are both accepted as well. Once the gate closes (usually around mid-October), there are no fees and you'll have to park in the winter lot.

A word of warning: all of the Brainard Lake parking lots fill up very early on summer/autumn weekends. I've seen packed lots at 5:30 am—assume they are full by 6:00 am. If you're

A unique look at Mount Toll from Little Pawnee's shoulder.

late, you'll either have to wait until a spot opens (which can literally take hours) or park in the winter lot and hike or bike in. Alternative strategies include hiking mid-week or reserving a camp spot at Pawnee Campground.

THE ROUTE: Enjoy a nice warm up along the nearly flat Long Lake Trail. At roughly 1.0 mile, as the trail begins to ascend near the west end of the lake, it's time to get off the trail and head up into the woods to your right (north). There's no "right" place to do this. I use a distinct gnarled tree at the top of a small hill as the entry point. Once off-trail, your goal is to hike up 0.75 mile to the open, broad east ridge of Little Pawnee Peak. There are animal trails through the forest and a bit of blowdown, but navigation is easy. Keep going up, trending a bit right (east) for the most open terrain. It's about 600 vertical feet to the clearings, where the route will become easy to follow.

Let the scrambling begin!

The wide-open plateau of the ridge feels like your own private mountain. This beautiful section of the

Some of the moves along the ridge are surprisingly exposed.

ridge eventually reaches 11,470 feet and is nearly flat for a few hundred feet. The ridge doesn't look so bad from here and it may be tough to actually tell what point is Little Pawnee Peak. Keep heading west for the big reveal.

Rings of black and brown rock announce the start of the Class 3 terrain. It's only 0.7 mile and about 900 vertical feet to the top from here but it will likely be slow moving. The challenge is to stay as close to the spine of the ridge as possible. The rock is very solid and staying on the ridge means scrambling on a few short catwalk sections with brief-but-real exposure. If there is any significant wind it will add to the thrill. Even though it's possible to retreat below the ridge at places, it's actually safer to stay on the ridge itself. It's Class 3 rock, albeit with a few heady sections. The closer you get to the notch, the wider the ridge becomes.

Just before the notch, the ridge broadens and you could just about hit the now-obvious summit of Little Pawnee Peak with a good frisbee throw. The crux notch itself is left of center. It is a 25-foot downclimb, best done with face-in climbing. There are good handholds and spotty footholds.

So is this crux Class 3 or Class 4? The answer is: both. If you're under 5'10" (like me), reaching down to the off-camber, grass foot ledges will mean stretching out full length

Looking down at the crux scramble.

to tap a toe down and slowly shift your weight. Because of the height and the pitch of the gully at the bottom, a fall here would mean serious trouble—thus the Class 4 assessment. A safety rope (30 meters is more than enough) is easily set up and is a very good idea for the under 6-foot crowd.

The closer to 6-feet you are, the easier this section is. A fellow 6'3" climber never had to straighten his arms to reach footholds that I, at 5'8", had to extend my arms to the max just to hover above. For him, it was easy Class 3. Use your best judgment here and if you have any apprehensions, setting up a rope and anchor will take very little time and offers a welcome margin of safety. Once in the notch itself, it's an easy Class 3 scramble up to the summit.

The register list showcases Little Pawnee Peak's introverted nature. From here, the ridge between Little Pawnee and Pawnee Peak is wickedly devious, decorated with cracked towers and crumbling walls. When you're ready, return the way you came. As is the case with many Class 3–4 options, the climb up the crux notch is easier than the climb down.

It's quickest and easiest to retrace your tracks through the woods and back toward Long Lake, though you do have the option of scaling down loose talus slopes into the basin between Blue Lake and Mitchell Lake, where the Mitchell Lake Trail will exit at the Mitchell Lake trailhead, necessitating a mile-long walk to the Long Lake trailhead. I prefer the Long Lake option—it is shorter, the footing is better, and you will likely encounter fewer people on the trail by virtue of being on the Long Lake Trail for only 1.0 mile. But if you want to stay out a bit longer and take in big views of Mount Toll and Paiute Peak from the Blue Lake basin, it is an option.

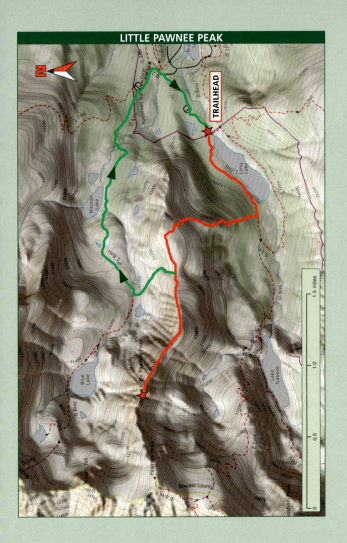

11. Blue Lake

RATING	Easy
ROUND-TRIP DISTANCE	4.8 miles
ROUND-TRIP TIME	2–4 hours
ELEVATION GAIN	920 feet
MAP	Trails Illustrated #102, Indian Peaks, Gold Hill; Latitude 40° Maps - Boulder County, Front Range
NEAREST LANDMARK	Ward

COMMENT: Yes, this is a popular hike and it is the most straightforward, on-trail walk in this guide. Far from being a secret, this may be the single most traveled trail in the Indian Peaks Wilderness. There is a good reason for this: the basin views of Mount Toll and Blue Lake are absolutely astounding. Framed by the shoulders of Mount Audubon, Paiute Peak, and Pawnee Peak's east ridge, it's one of the most impressive amphitheaters in the Rocky Mountains. Water seeps from the headwalls of Mount Toll and snow patches merge with green bands of pine trees to create a powerful landscape. It is one of those destinations that is worth visiting in different seasons.

Mount Audubon from Mitchell Lake.

A dreamscape sky. PHOTO BY DEBBIE BRUGGEMAN   Cascading spring runoff.

There is nothing complicated or hidden about Blue Lake (11,309 feet). It's simply one of the prettiest spots in the entire Indian Peaks and it just happens to be quite accessible. In spring, this is a popular trail for backcountry skiers as the east face of Mount Toll is prime backcountry terrain. It is possible to climb Mount Toll from this basin on Class 2, loose scree slopes.

GETTING THERE: The hike begins at the Mitchell Lake trailhead located within Brainard Lake Recreation Area. The turnoff to Brainard Lake Road is off CO-72 (Peak-to-Peak Highway) in Ward. From Nederland, this is 11.8 miles from the round-about turn onto CO-72. It's also possible to get here by driving up Left Hand Canyon, through Ward, and turning right onto CO-72. The left (west) turn to the well-marked Brainard Lake Road is about 200 feet past the junction of CO-72 and the top of Left Hand Canyon Drive (called Nelson Road on some maps).

Brainard Lake Road was repaved and improved in 2018, making for a smooth ride. It's 2.5 miles to the toll gate/winter parking lot, then another 2.8 miles to the Mitchell Lake trailhead. Note this access road was re-routed south along Brainard Lake. Follow it to the parking lot at the end of the road.

As of 2019, it is $11 per vehicle / $6 for motorcycle / $1 for pedestrians and cyclists for a 3-day pass. The America the Beautiful Pass and the American Land & Leisure Pass are both accepted as well. Once the gate closes (usually around mid-October), there are no fees and you'll have to park in the winter lot.

Mount Toll standing guard over Blue Lake.
PHOTO BY DEBBI BRUGGEMAN

A word of warning: all of the Brainard Lake parking lots fill up very early on summer/autumn weekends. I've seen packed lots at 5:30 am—assume they are full by 6:00 am. If you're late, you'll either have to wait until a spot opens (which can literally take hours) or park in the winter lot and hike or bike in. Alternative strategies include hiking mid-week or reserving a camp spot at Pawnee Campground.

THE ROUTE: From the Mitchell Lake trailhead, head west on the Mitchell Lake Trail. It's strange that both the trailhead and main trail out of the lot are named for Mitchell Lake, which is a fine little lake but not nearly as significant a destination as Blue Lake or Mount Audubon (which it shares a trailhead with). An easy mile brings you to Mitchell Lake, which has a quaint, understated presence in this land of giants. Mount Audubon's south slopes loom large, as does Little Pawnee/Pawnee Peak's north slopes and cliffs. After passing Mitchell Lake, treeline fades into shrub line and streaks of creeks start to appear, supplying clear pools and nurturing wildflowers. Continue another 1.2 miles on the trail.

As the basin opens up, there is a neat natural feature just before Blue Lake. Something like a horizontal waterfall, comprised of rock-block steps flows from above. Blue Lake is quite an amazing sight, especially if the clouds play with the shadows that dance over the land. This is a good place to sit, relax, and enjoy a spectacular setting. Return when you are ready.

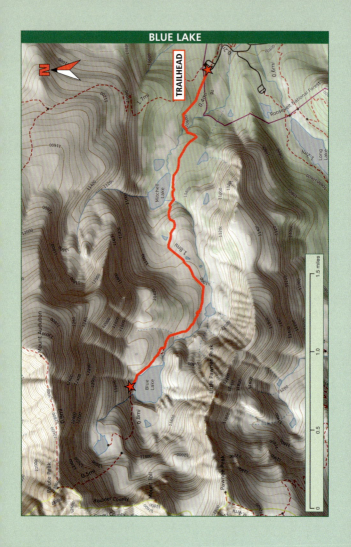

BLUE LAKE

TRAILHEAD

Roosevelt National Forest

Mitchell Lake

1.8mi

Blue Lake

Mount Audubon

Little Pawnee Peak

Pawnee Peak

Mount Toll

Boulder County

1.5 miles

1.0

0.5

0

12. Navajo Peak

RATING	Difficult
ROUND-TRIP DISTANCE	8.9 miles
ROUND-TRIP TIME	6.5–8 hours
ELEVATION GAIN	2,825 feet
MAP	Trails Illustrated #102, Indian Peaks, Gold Hill; Latitude 40° Maps - Boulder County, Front Range
NEAREST LANDMARK	Ward

COMMENT: Navajo Peak's 13,409-foot summit pyramid is the third tallest and one of the most distinct mountain profiles in the IPW. The hike to the top involves a scrappy off-trail trek through a rocky basin, a scramble up a loose couloir, and a gutsy Class 3 climb to a tiny summit. But perhaps more noteworthy is the plane wreckage strewn throughout the route. Airplane Gully derives its name from the January 21, 1948 crash of a C-47 that claimed the lives of three men. Much of the debris is still on the mountain, including the large fuselage section near the top of Airplane Gully.

Besides the novelty of the wreckage, it's worth noting that this isn't the easiest way up Navajo Peak but it is the easiest

Airplane Gully is the snow-free ramp left of center.

legal way. Navajo's northeast ridge (Niwot Ridge) crosses into the forbidden Boulder Watershed, where public traffic is illegal. Several gorgeous lakes and three prominent IPW summits (Kiowa Peak, Arikaree Peak, and Mount Albion) are trapped in this closed-off region. As of 2019, there are no plans to open these peaks to the public so you'll have to enjoy them from afar while exploring Navajo Peak.

Wreckage along the way.

The off-trail navigation from the Isabelle Glacier Trail to the summit is only about 1.0 mile, but it will require a skilled eye. If there are spring snowfields, travel may be easier or harder depending on if you punch through the snow. Even though the summit block scramble is airy, the correct line will stay solid Class 3. The 13,140-foot tower perched above Navajo Glacier is known as Dicker's Peak because Colorado's founding climbers were delightfully immature.

GETTING THERE: Navajo Peak starts from the Long Lake trailhead at the Brainard Lake Recreation Area (which is also the jumping off point to two other hikes in this guide). The turnoff to Brainard Lake Road is off CO-72 (Peak-to-Peak Highway) in Ward. From Nederland, this is 11.8 miles from the roundabout onto CO-72. It's also possible to get here by driving up Left Hand Canyon, through Ward, and turning right onto CO-72. The left (west) turn to the well-marked Brainard Lake Road is about 200 feet past the junction of CO-72 and the top of Left Hand Canyon Drive (called Nelson Road on some maps).

Brainard Lake Road was repaved and improved in 2018, making for a smooth ride. It's 2.5 miles to the toll gate/winter parking lot, then another 2.5 miles to the Long Lake

Navajo (center). The cheeky Dicker's Peck spire can be seen above the Navajo Snowfield.

trailhead. Note this access road was recently re-routed south along Brainard Lake. Follow the road around the lake to the west side, then take a left onto the well-marked road to the trailhead.

As of 2019, it is $11 per vehicle / $6 for motorcycle / $1 for pedestrians and cyclists for a 3-day pass. The America the Beautiful Pass and the American Land & Leisure Pass are both accepted as well. Once the gate closes (usually around mid-October), there are no fees and you'll have to park in the winter lot.

A word of warning: all of the Brainard Lake parking lots fill up very early on summer/autumn weekends. I've seen packed lots at 5:30 am—assume they are full by 6:00 am. If you're late, you'll either have to wait until a spot opens (which can literally take hours) or park in the winter lot and hike or bike in. Alternative strategies include hiking mid-week or reserving a camp spot at Pawnee Campground.

THE ROUTE: From the Long Lake trailhead, hike on the Long Lake Trail for 1.1 miles, where it turns into the Pawnee Pass Trail and trends toward Isabelle Lake. Stay on the Pawnee

Pass Trail for 0.8 mile. At Lake Isabelle, hop off the Paw-nee Pass Trail and take the Isabelle Glacier Trail. You have another 1.5 miles to go before getting off-trail.

After 3.5 miles, at 11,500 feet near a marshy section, it's time to go off-trail. You'll see the rocky basin below, but don't go all the way down. Your goal is to trend toward a small shelf below Navajo Glacier, between the summits of Navajo and Apache Peaks. Using Navajo itself as a point of refer-ence, you'll be aiming for the couloirs left of center, which is of course far left of the glacier/snowfield. If in doubt, keep trending toward the central flanks of Navajo Peak.

At 12,280 feet, you'll find yourself at the base of a pair of gullies on the north face of Navajo Peak. Scan left from the summit pyramid. The first prominent gully to the left of the summit is not the one you're looking for. Scan past a prow of rock left to see Airplane Gully. There are two clues that this is the correct gully. The first is that the spread of boulders at the bottom is less steep and rockier than the first gully. Sec-ondly, you'll likely see glints of metal leading up like a trail of ghostly breadcrumbs. Wreckage is strewn throughout the gully, including some fairly large and intact pieces.

This gully gains 900 vertical feet in less than 0.5 mile and is very loose in places. There is no real exposure, but the Class 2+ scramble is on some rotten rock. About halfway up, the gully forks—veer right. At nearly the top of the gully at 12,900 feet is the largest piece of wreckage. A significant portion of the fuselage sits in lonely decay, with flowers occa-

The easiest scrambling is found on the left (south) side of the summit block.

Unique rock formation just below the summit block.

sionally sprouting between its rusty gears. Past this, continue a short distance and exit the gully onto Niwot Ridge.

Topping out on the gully, head west toward the intimidating summit block. There doesn't appear to be an easy way up, but don't lose heart. Trend left (south) around the block until you see a notable stem of rock known as the Monkey Fist below you at roughly 13,300 feet. To your right and slightly above you are the Class 3 sections that scramble about 40 feet to the summit block. The rock here is good and the exposure is significant. Push onto the top, which only has room for about two people.

Navajo's wild summit will make your heart race. Chances are you won't linger too long, given the sparse real estate available. When you're ready to descend, return the way you came, taking extra care to downclimb off the summit block. Also, make sure that you descend the correct gully on the way down (you may want to leave a temporary marker at the top of Airplane Gully to ensure you return the correct way). Going down the gully is a slog, so take it easy. You'll have a decent visual guide back to Lake Isabelle, so bear toward it to reconnect to the Isabelle Glacier Trail and the way back home.

13. Arapaho Peaks

RATING	South Arapaho Peak, Moderate; North Arapaho Peak, Difficult
ROUND-TRIP DISTANCE	South Arapaho Peak, 8 miles; North Arapaho Peak, 9.2 miles
ROUND-TRIP TIME	South Arapaho Peak 6–7 hours; North Arapaho Peak 7–9 hours
ELEVATION GAIN	3,650 feet
MAP	Trails Illustrated #102, Indian Peaks, Gold Hill; Latitude 40° Maps - Boulder County, Front Range * Boulder Nederland
NEAREST LANDMARK	Town of Eldora

COMMENT: An audience with the king of the Indian Peaks is not easily won. The 13,502-foot North Arapaho Peak is the highest point in the IPW and this thrilling traverse is the least difficult way to the top. The 0.75-mile ridge connecting the two Arapaho Peaks packs a lot of challenge in a short distance, including a 10-foot-tall rock slab, an airy catwalk, tricky route finding, and semi-hidden downclimbs. Bring your A-Game if you wish to stand upon its broad, spacious summit, topped with a large, crowning cairn.

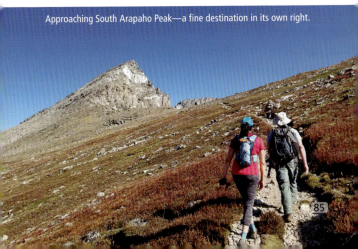

Approaching South Arapaho Peak—a fine destination in its own right.

Old ruins from the 4th of July mine.

Excellent rock awaits on the traverse.

The more accommodating South Arapaho Peak (13,397 feet) is the gateway to the traverse and is a fine out-and-back, non-technical hike on its own. Despite not being an officially ranked Colorado summit (due to its lack of prominence from the taller North Arapaho Peak), most hikers agree that South Arapaho is the more visually impressive mountain. It cuts an imposing, jagged profile when seen from the 12,720-foot saddle on the approach. Below the traverse is the fast-receding Arapaho Glacier, the largest in the state of Colorado. It is within a section of the City of Boulder's watershed that is off-limits to non-authorized visitors. Both Arapaho Peak summits are also within the perplexing watershed boundary but legal to visit.

The traverse should take average, fit hikers with good route finding skills 45 minutes to an hour each way. If the weather looks iffy, don't push your luck—there are no good bailout routes on the traverse. Oddly, the traverse ridge isn't the boundary of the Boulder watershed, though you will be bouncing over the line between Boulder and Grand Counties that *is* defined by the ridge.

One last note: this is *not* a dog-friendly traverse. While there are certainly some dogs that are capable, there is a lot of fall potential and bringing along your pup is strongly discouraged. If you need a little extra dog mileage, try adding Old Baldy to a summit of South Arapaho.

GETTING THERE: This hike begins at the Fourth of July trailhead, named for the Fourth of July Mine, whose steampunk ruins can be seen 2.0 miles into the hike. This may be the

Midway through the traverse.

boldest mountain road a Honda Civic can conquer—it's bumpy, but the trailhead is reachable by most passenger cars.

From the tiny town of Nederland, take CO-119 south and proceed through town to the well-signed right turn to Eldora Road toward Eldora Ski area. If approaching from CO-119 north, this well-marked turn will be on your left just before entering Nederland. Follow Eldora Road for 4.0 miles, ignoring the turnoff for Eldora Ski Area. Pass slowly through the even tinier town of Eldora, which makes Nederland look like a booming metropolis in comparison. At 4.0 miles, the road turns to dirt just before the chaotic Hessie trailhead. Continue 0.8 mile and bear right onto Fourth of July Road. Continue 3.8 miles (4.6 miles total from the start of the dirt) as the rocky road climbs along a few dramatic shelf-road sections to the trailhead, just past Buckingham Campground. There are two main parking areas that share a restroom. If you arrive after 6:30 am most summer days, expect to park along the road. Please respect the marked private driveways in the area.

THE ROUTE: From the upper trailhead parking, begin your adventure along the well-traveled Arapaho Pass Trail. Gradu-

That's quite a cairn on the summit of North Arapahoe Peak!

ally climb through vanilla-scented pine forests as the high ridges that frame the valley slowly reveal themselves. At 1.2 miles, stay on the Arapaho Pass Trail where it merges with the Diamond Lake Trail. From here, views begin to expand and showcase the majesty of the Indian Peaks—12,814-foot Mount Neva dominates the horizon. At 2.0 miles, reach a flat, open meadow that features a network of small, clear pools before reaching a few rusted mining relics and the junction with the Arapaho Glacier Trail. South Arapaho Peak looms imposingly to the north.

At a sandy section just before the old mining pumps and gears, turn right onto the Arapaho Glacier Trail. Go slightly downhill to an easy river crossing. Past this crossing, the trail is temporarily swallowed by willows. Keep your eyes down to find the path and mash your way a few hundred feet through the marsh, where the trail will reappear in full figure. At 3.6 miles, you'll reach the 12,720-foot saddle between South Arapaho Peak and 13,038-foot Old Baldy (a nice optional summit that is 0.4 mile east of the saddle). Views down to the grizzled Arapaho Glacier come into full focus. The last 0.4 mile up South Arapaho's southeast ridge presents the biggest challenge thus far. The fierce, shattered crags on South Arapaho's east face offers a dramatic photo background.

The intermittent trail up the ridge never surpasses Class 2 in difficulty, though the path does dissolve in some of the rockier sections. Stay close to the ridge, nudging left off-ridge where needed. A few easy scrambling moves on solid rock are required before reaching the summit 4.0 miles in. If South Arapaho Peak was your goal for the day, retrace your steps after you've had your fill of the summit. One quick tip: there are a few informal trails that break off right between the summit and a small, 13,320-foot false summit. Ignore these and descend the ridge back to the saddle before heading down.

If you're continuing onto North Arapaho Peak, be certain the weather is not threatening—you *really* don't want to get caught by a storm up here since you must return the way you came. The ridge is only 0.7 mile long and can be seen in its entirety from South Arapaho. The devil, of course, is in the details. Start by descending northwest along the easy, stable ridge. As the ridge begins to bend to the north, the trail breaks from the crest and dips left (west) and below a troublesome, exposed notch along the ridge proper. Several of these notches stymie a straight run on the ridge and will require down-climbed detours ahead. Note there are several faded orange dots and arrows that disguise them-

More great scrambling.

Eyeing up the traverse on the return to South Arapahoe Peak.

The easiest line often drops west of the ridge proper.

selves as alpine lichen along the way. They only offer intermittent guidance so don't rely on them, but be aware they roughly tag the most logical way across.

Now the real fun begins. Follow the trail and a few makeshift cairns up to your right into a protected notch to a 10-foot slab that regains the ridge. Despite a somewhat notorious reputation, this obstacle requires a single move and is not highly exposed—yet. There are small but solid footholds on the slab and a good staging rock just off to the right. For those over 6 feet tall, the move is an absolute breeze. My climbing partner is 5'4" and she had no problem with the move. It's easy Class 4 for most climbers. On the return, the downclimb is relatively easy.

Past the slab is the headiest section of the traverse, a dizzying 25-foot long narrow catwalk on excellent rock with wild exposure. There's no shame in butt-shuffling along this short section, especially if there is wind or snow present. Past this, the route finding becomes more challenging. Staying high on the ridge (or just off the west side of the ridge) is possible, as the rock is quite good and this is the Class 4 option. Most people will detour left (west) as there are easier Class 3 lines west of the ridge. The first of these will require a face-in downclimb of about 35 feet on very good rock with good footing. It's easy to keep it at Class 3, but locating the best downclimb chutes and ledges can be intimidating at first glance. Continue undulating in this fashion. Aim to stay high on the ridge when you can, detouring and downclimbing to the west when you get notched out.

For many, this short slab is the crux of the traverse.

The final approach finds the ridge blocked by another deep notch. Downclimbing one more time on the west side is a bit heady here and requires good route finding and face-in descending. After reaching a final saddle before the summit block, the route to the top looks fairly desperate—the only obvious exit appears to be a chock-stoned gully left of a deep fissure that splits the face. This is not the way up, but it's the right way to trend. Start left on good rock until you are near the base of the fissure. A hidden and welcome band of light-colored rock ascends right on good rock to a small, shadowy notch right of the smooth-ish block face. At the top of this wide slope is a single step east over a mini-ridge to an off-camber patch of powder-white rock. Pass this small step with care and scramble up the mercifully protected shadowy notch to a glorious, flat walk to the summit cairn.

Your work isn't over. The return north to south is somewhat easier, as the route is visually more open and scrambling up the previously downclimbed sections is easier for most climbers. And you've already climbed it once. The exposed catwalk, perhaps the mental crux of the traverse, is more daunting but just as solid. Lower yourself past the slab and remember to stay right (west) and avoid the ridge until you've turned slightly southeast back toward South Arapaho. The final hike on the easier terrain back up South Arapaho is a great relief from the vigilant route finding on the traverse. Remember not to take any of the aforementioned side trails on the face of South Arapaho on the descent, staying close to the ridge until reaching the saddle with Old Baldy.

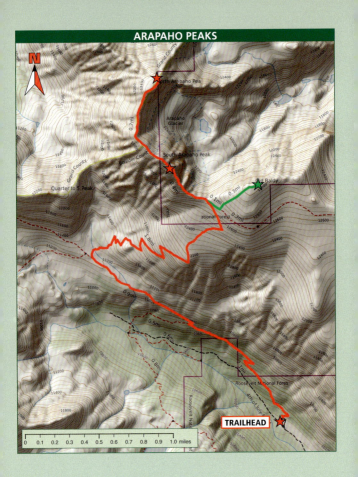

TRAILHEAD

0 0.1 0.2 0.3 0.4 0.5 0.6 0.7 0.8 0.9 1.0 miles

THE BEST INDIAN PEAKS WILDERNESS HIKES

14. Lake Dorothy

RATING	Easy to Moderate
ROUND-TRIP DISTANCE	6.5 miles
ROUND-TRIP TIME	3–5 hours
ELEVATION GAIN	2,030 feet
BONUS	Quarter to 5 Peak—12,300 feet
MAP	Trails Illustrated #102, Indian Peaks, Gold Hill; Latitude 40° Maps - Boulder County, Boulder Nederland
NEAREST LANDMARK	Town of Eldora

COMMENT: Lake Dorothy (12,067 feet) sits below Mount Neva's imposing north ridge, a tranquil counterpart to the craggy ridgeline. This wide-open alpine lake sits just past Arapaho Pass and is a great destination for a day-hike that offers a good balance of fitness and fun. En route to the lake, hikers pass the ruins of the Fourth of July Mine, including an old boiler and other intact artifacts. Those looking to add a little extra to their day can continue along the shelf-cut Caribou Pass Trail and steal a glimpse into the western Indian Peaks Wilderness.

Lake Dorothy. PHOTO BY DEBBI BRUGGEMAN

Caribou Lake from Arapahoe Pass.

This is a great hike for groups of varying abilities or for those who simply want to enjoy a little lake time in the mountains. Peakbaggers have the option of taking on a fun Class 2+ scramble 0.8 mile (one-way) to 12,300-foot Quarter to 5 Peak, a quirky little summit that is a nice contrast to the more challenging peaks in the area. Because the Fourth of July trailhead services a lot of terrain, expect a modest amount of traffic up to the Fourth of July Mine. Beyond that, the crowds disperse as you get farther west.

GETTING THERE: This hike begins at the Fourth of July trailhead. The road in is bumpy but attainable by carefully driven passenger cars.

From the tiny town of Nederland, take CO-119 south and proceed through town to the well-signed right turn to Eldora Road toward Eldora Ski area. If approaching from CO-119 north, this well-marked turn will be on your left just before entering Nederland. Follow Eldora Road for 4.0 miles, ignoring the turnoff for Eldora Ski Area. Pass slowly through the even tinier town of Eldora, which makes Nederland look like a booming metropolis in comparison. At 4.0 miles, the road turns to dirt just before the chaotic Hessie trailhead. Continue 0.8 mile and bear right onto Fourth of July Road. Continue 3.8 miles (4.6 miles total from the start of the dirt) as the rocky road climbs along a few dramatic shelf-road sec-

Along the Arapahoe Pass Trail.   Lake Dorothy in the distance, seen from North Arapaho Peak.

tions to the trailhead, just past Buckingham Campground. There are two main parking areas that share a restroom. If you arrive after 6:30 am most summer days, expect to park along the road. Please respect the marked private driveways in the area.

THE ROUTE: Start at the Fourth of July trailhead on the Arapaho Pass Trail. This hike is on-trail all the way to the lake, so enjoy the gradual climb up past creeks, knobby pine trees, and eventually above treeline. In 2.0 miles, at a marshy clearing, the majesty of the high peaks in the basin is in full view. This is the old Fourth of July Mine site and there are a lot of relics out in the open. Moose are common in this area. Continue on the Arapaho Pass Trail another 1.1 miles as it traverses below Quarter to 5 Peak toward Arapaho Pass.

At Arapaho Pass, Lake Dorothy is just a few hundred feet away. Views north to Caribou Lake and the accompanying peaks in the distance highlight the less hectic vibe of the western IPW. It's worth wandering out on the Caribou Pass Trail west. The sidecut trail is relatively level and the views west are wonderful. When you're ready, take the Arapaho Pass Trail back to the parking area.

Quarter to 5 Peak: This delightful Class 2+ scramble is 1.6 miles out-and-back from Arapaho Pass. From Arapaho Pass, simply take the ridge east up past a false summit and along a narrow but not wildly exposed ridge to the summit. At 12,300 feet, it's far from the biggest mountain in the area and is easy to overlook, but the scramble is quite a fun outing.

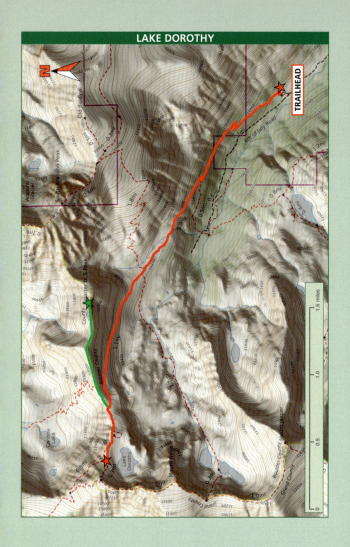

15. Needle's Eye Tunnel

RATING	Easy
ROUND-TRIP DISTANCE	3.5 miles from Jenny Lake; 5.6 miles from Forest Lakes trailhead
ROUND-TRIP TIME	1.5 hours from Jenny Lake / 2.5 hours from Forest Lakes
ELEVATION GAIN	945 feet from Jenny Lake; 847 feet from Forest Lakes trailhead
BONUS	Mount Epworth 11,843 feet; Forest Lakes 10,287 feet
MAP	Trails Illustrated #103, Winter Park, Central City, Rollins Pass; Latitude 40° Maps - Front Range
NEAREST LANDMARK	Moffat Tunnel

COMMENT: The narrow Needle's Eye Tunnel (11,385 feet) was the crowning achievement of another era. Visits to the ambitious (and short-lived) town of Corona (11,660 feet) via railroad was once one of Colorado's most memorable and exciting adventures. Though the tunnel is now fenced off, the area is rich with history, along with exceptional views along both sides of the Continental Divide. It boggles the mind to think of trains running year-round over Rollins Pass Road

Jenny Lake.

at the beginning of the last century. This hike begins east of Needle's Eye Tunnel then goes up and over to the west side of the Divide. Along the way, you pass ancient stone walls that native hunters used to funnel migrating elk into hunting traps and the ruins of the buildings that once stood atop Rollins Pass. For those looking for more adventure, nearby Mount Epworth is a delightful, easily attained summit.

The rich history of Rollins Pass is more than this humble guidebook can cover. If you'd like to read more, *Rollins Pass* (B. Travis Wright and Kate Wright; 2018, Arcadia Publishing) is a well-researched resource.

After rounding the tunnel, there are nice views of King's Lake and the Bob and Betty Lakes (page 103), as well as 12,383-foot Skyscraper Peak.

GETTING THERE: From the town of Rollinsville off CO-119, turn west onto East Portal Road/Tolland Road. Follow this highly maintained dirt road 7.5 miles west to the hairpin turn onto the rocky, railroad grade Moffat Road (aka Rollins Pass Road). This bumpy, slow-driving road is passable for SUVs and carefully driven sport utility cars like Subaru Outbacks. Passenger cars are not advised and will take an absolute beating. It's 8.8 miles up to the first parking area at Yankee Doodle Lake, but for these hikes, you'll want to drive farther—if you can. In many years, a snowdrift blocks the road above Yankee Doodle Lake until mid-June. If so, you'll have to park at Yankee Doodle Lake and walk 0.7 mile to the Jenny Lake trailhead.

However, once the snow has melted, you have two parking options. The first is the aforementioned 0.7 mile up to Jenny Lake trailhead, which is the ultra-direct way to the Needle's Eye Tunnel via a very steep, short hill hike. The brief entrance to this parking area is rutted out and may be too much for lower clearance vehicles, although you can easily park at the turnoff itself and spare your vehicle.

The other option is to drive 0.9 mile past the Jenny Lake trailhead to the Forest Lakes trailhead. This small parking area has spots for 6 cars and roadside parking. This option is nice if you want to make the short 0.5-mile hike down to the

The Needle's Eye Tunnel will likely be closed for the foreseeable future.

highest of the Forest Lakes on the Forest Lakes Trail. Sport utility cars can make this trailhead.

THE ROUTE: If you started at Jenny Lake, the Needle's Eye Tunnel is 0.3 mile above you, roughly 400 vertical feet, directly up a steep slope with a few improvised trails. Near the top, this slope is loose but manageable. It connects with the top of Moffat Road, delivering you to the fenced-off Needle's Eye Tunnel. This hill is strenuous, but for fit hikers it's the quickest way to the tunnel.

If you start at the Forest Lakes trailhead, you're in for a treat. It's a 0.9-mile walk north along the upper portion of Moffat Road. Just past the trailhead, the road is intentionally blocked to vehicles by boulders in a narrow gap carved out over a hundred years ago. Imagine the work to blast through that solid rock! The walk from here to Needle's Eye Tunnel is pleasant and easy along the wide road.

Using the Forest Lakes trailhead mileage, you'll be at the Needle's Eye Tunnel in 2.8 miles. The tunnel was restored in the late 1980s but permanently closed in 1990 due to rockfall in the tunnel. Reopening the tunnel remains a controversial issue but as of 2019, it remains sealed off.

Before hiking on, a little history. The original Moffat Road was built in 1862 for wagon traffic, then improved to host

Mount Epworth from the old Corona town site.

a railroad in 1880. The tunnel was completed in 1903. The unbelievable town of Corona was built as a waypoint for trains and the travelers in 1904 and most of the structures (including the train station) were covered by wooden shelters. To hike over the tunnel, follow the obvious trail to the right of the fenced-off entrance and over. Above the tunnel are several elaborate rock shelters. Some archaeologists believe these were originally built by Paleo-Indians over 3,200 years ago.

Back to the hike. Hoof over the tunnel passage and either descend down to the north side of the tunnel and the road or take a hiking trail along the slopes—both are fun. From here, it's roughly 1.8 miles to the Corona townsite. The old trestle is still intact (though rotting out) along the way. Views here are spectacular. The small corridor between the Indian Peaks and James Peak Wilderness areas isn't marked, but there is a small gap between the two that is merely the Roosevelt National Forest.

As you round the bend, surprise! There's a parking lot here for cars coming up the western segment of the Moffat Road from Winter Park. The ruins of Corona are here … sort of. Even the ruins are ruined. When the Moffat Tunnel (down at the East Portal trailhead) was completed in 1928, Corona's days were numbered. Train tracks were left in place until 1935 as an emergency route—the same year that what was

Epworth's summit.   The open alpine tundra above Jenny Lake.

left of Corona burned down. The road itself was retrofit for auto traffic in 1955 and by that time, the Corona ruins were all but forgotten. There's not much to see. Old timbers, a few foundations, and the odd bolt here and there. Yet, it's still a beautiful place to visit and there are many informational signs to read about the history of the area.

Return when you are ready, either over the high ridge or along the road again. Your mileage may vary depending on how much you wander around, but this is all easy walking and exploring.

Mount Epworth: 11,843-foot Mount Epworth is one of my absolute favorite summits in Colorado. It's rather inconspicuous, but it has great views, a fun scramble, and has an intangible charm that has brought me to its summit many times. The caveat here: it's not in the James Peak or Indian Peak Wilderness. But since you're here … you may want to check it out. From the Corona townsite parking on the west side of Moffat Road, it's roughly 1.3 miles one-way to the summit. Walk south down the road, then head off-trail to Pumphouse Lake at the foot of Mount Epworth, then scramble up the north slopes (Class 2+). The elevation gain is 540 feet one-way, so a modest 2.6 miles extra to your day.

Forest Lakes: Parking at the Forest Lakes trailhead gives you quick, easy access down to the highest of the Forest Lakes (less than 0.5 mile on an established, signed trail). It's a nice add-on to your day, especially if the summer sun is burning hot.

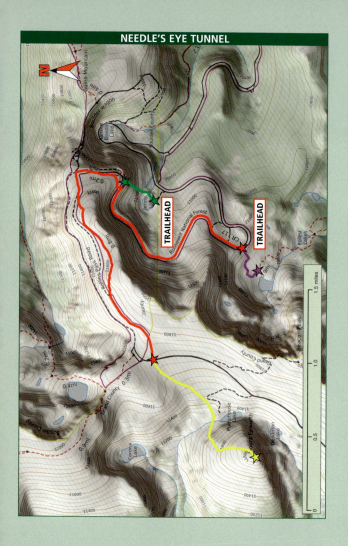

THE BEST INDIAN PEAKS WILDERNESS HIKES

16. Bob and Betty Lakes

RATING	Easy
ROUND-TRIP DISTANCE	4.1 miles
ROUND-TRIP TIME	2–4 hours
ELEVATION GAIN	1,060 feet
MAPS	Trails Illustrated Map #102, Indian Peaks, Gold Hill; #103, Winter Park, Central City, Rollins Pass; Latitude 40° Maps - Front Range
NEAREST LANDMARK	Moffat Tunnel

COMMENT: This is the rare hike that begins downhill! It's possible to reach Bob Lake (11,575 feet) and Betty Lake (11,450 feet) from the east via the Hessie trailhead, though it's quite a long day (close to 13 miles round-trip) and you'll have to contend with finding a parking spot and on summer weekends, possibly having to take a shuttle from Nederland just to reach Hessie trailhead. This route, however, starts from the Rollins Pass trailhead reached via the western side of the Moffat Road. It gives you all the glory without nearly as much of the grit! You'll park at the old Corona townsite before descending down to King Lake and over to Betty and Bob Lakes.

Bob Lake. PHOTO BY DEBBI BRUGGEMAN

King Lake. PHOTO BY DEBBI BRUGGEMAN

Explorers can get a lot out of this area. It's easy enough to walk around to the Needle's Eye Tunnel, scramble up Mount Epworth (page 101 for details on these hikes), or simply walk along the Continental Divide. Detours aside, the beauty of these three lakes is exquisite. Wildflowers can flood the tundra with color in late spring and early summer and the hilltop above Bob Lake has one of my favorite informal names in the Indian Peaks Wilderness: Bob Knob.

Mount Epworth, not technically in the IPW or James Peak Wilderness, is nonetheless a fun scramble. The 12,014-foot point just east of the parking area has a unique spot where Boulder, Gilpin, and Grand Counties intersect, though it's not marked. It is fun to wander up to the ridge, but if you have pups in tow be aware that the east face of this ridge cliffs out in places.

GETTING THERE: From US -40 in Winter Park, turn east onto the signed Rollins Pass Road (FSR 149/CO-Road 80). This road is located between the Winter Park Ski area entrance and the town of Winter Park. Then it's a 13.8-mile bump-fest up to the Rollins Pass trailhead parking area. It's not quite as rugged as the eastern side of the pass (Moffat Road) and passenger cars can make it up if carefully driven. There is plenty of parking at the top.

PHOTO BY DEBBI BRIGGEMAN

THE ROUTE: Even before you hike a single step, the views are incredible. There are informational signs and the sparse ruins of the town of Corona. The King Lake Trail begins to the northwest of the lot at an Indian Peaks Wilderness boundary sign. Take the King Lake Trail north and downhill to your first

Betty lake. PHOTO BY DEBBI BRIGGEMAN

goal, King Lake (11,437 feet), which is quickly reached and might just be enough to satisfy your lake cravings. Flowers ring the lake into late summer. Continue north on King Lake Trail, passing a side trail to a small tarn to the north (an easy detour for the curious).

In 0.9 mile, reach the signed turn for the Bob and Betty Lakes Trail. Head north 0.7 mile, gaining about 400 feet of elevation to Betty Lake, which is the more photogenic of the two folksy-named lakes. To reach Bob Lake, follow the faint trail northwest up the drainage. Bob Lake is a peaceful place, though more enclosed than Betty Lake. Unlike most hikes, you'll have to ascend another 500+ vertical feet on the way back. Return the way you came when you're ready to go.

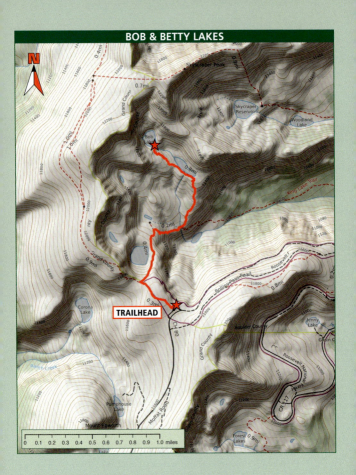

BOB & BETTY LAKES

N

Skyscraper Peak

Skyscraper
Reservoir

Woodland
Lake

King Lake Trail

Bob
Lake

0.8mi

0.7mi

0.4mi

0.2mi

Roosevelt

Rolling Pass Road

0.8mi

0.3mi

TRAILHEAD

Corona
Lake

Jenny
Lake

Glenn

Boulder County

Grand County

Roosevelt National

Ranch Creek

Pumphouse
Lake

Mortal Forks

CR 117

Mount Eoworth

Forest 0.9mi
Lakes

| 0 | 0.1 | 0.2 | 0.3 | 0.4 | 0.5 | 0.6 | 0.7 | 0.8 | 0.9 | 1.0 miles |

17. Diamond Lake

RATING	Easy
ROUND-TRIP DISTANCE	5.4 miles
ROUND-TRIP TIME	3–4 hours
ELEVATION GAIN	900 feet
MAP	Trails Illustrated #103, Winter Park, Central City, Rollins Pass; Latitude 40° Maps - Front Range
NEAREST LANDMARK	Town of Eldora

COMMENT: Diamond Lake is a gorgeous forest pool that is the perfect destination for a casual day out. Even though it stays below treeline, the trail to Diamond Lake follows creeks, waterfalls, and mossy woods, offering a different look at the Indian Peaks Wilderness. Views from the lake are beautifully framed by Jasper Peak's long-reaching southeast ridge. Adventurous explorers can follow the creeks that drain into Diamond Lake west into the basin for a little off-trail fun.

Many people pair Diamond Lake with a trip to the Fourth of July Mine ruins on the Arapaho Pass Trail. This is done by visiting Diamond Lake first, then returning to the Arapaho Pass Trail and going west roughly 1.0 mile to the clearing where the mine ruins sit just beside the trail. This adds 2.0 total miles to the day, but it is all on-trail and will only add about an hour to your outing.

Diamond Lake's peaceful shores.
PHOTO BY DEBBI BRUGGEMAN

Wildflowers. BY DEBBI BRUGGEMAN

GETTING THERE: This hike begins at the Fourth of July trailhead. The road in is bumpy but attainable by carefully driven passenger cars.

From the tiny town of Nederland, take CO-119 south and proceed through town to the well-signed right turn to Eldora Road toward Eldora Ski area. If approaching from CO-119 north, this well-marked turn will be on your left just before entering Nederland. Follow Eldora Road for 4.0 miles, ignoring the turnoff for Eldora Ski Area. Pass slowly through the even tinier town of Eldora, which makes Nederland look like a booming metropolis in comparison. At 4.0 miles, the road turns to dirt just before the chaotic Hessie trailhead. Continue 0.8 mile and bear right onto the Fourth of July Road. Continue 3.8 miles (4.6 miles total from the start of the dirt) as the rocky road climbs along a few dramatic shelf-road sections to the trailhead, just past Buckingham Campground. There are two main parking areas that share a restroom. If you arrive after 6:30 am most summer days, expect to park along the road. Please respect the marked private driveways in the area.

THE ROUTE: Start on the Arapaho Pass Trail at the upper parking area at the Fourth of July trailhead (near the restrooms) and follow it 1.0 mile to the junction with the Diamond Lake Trail. Turn left onto the Diamond Lake Trail. Head downhill, cross a few bridges and follow the trail through the woods. After 0.5 mile, the trail begins to climb again, gradually gaining over 400 vertical feet en route to the lake, which is reached at 2.7 miles. Relax and enjoy the views west, where the landscape transforms from forest to alpine mountain. On a day with little wind, the lake is strikingly clear. Boulders that decorate the shallows are a nice touch to the scene. When you're ready, return the way you came.

N

TRAILHEAD

0.5 miles
0.4
0.3
0.2
0.1
0

Arapaho Pass Trail #904

4th of July Road

1.1mi

0.5mi

0.8mi

0.4mi

18. James Peak

RATING	Moderate
ROUND-TRIP DISTANCE	7.2 miles
ROUND-TRIP TIME	4.5–6 hours
ELEVATION GAIN	2,950 feet
MAP	Trails Illustrated #103, Winter Park, Central City, Rollins Pass; Latitude 40° Maps - Front Range
NEAREST LANDMARK	St. Marys Glacier

COMMENT: The tastefully named James Peak (13,294 feet) is the namesake summit of the James Peak Wilderness and a fine 13er for a day hike. The standard route goes by St. Marys Lake and St. Marys Glacier, one of the most accessible glaciers in the state (though it will likely melt out in the next decade). Above the glacier, an expanse of alpine tundra bridges the gap between the final climb to the summit.

This is a popular hike and a good first summit for those looking to get a taste of IPW peak bagging. Nearby Kingston Peak (12,043 feet) offers a bonus destination that is an easy add-on. For more casual hikers, simply going to the base of the glacier has its own allure.

In the middle of the open tundra between Lunch Rock and James Peak is a 4x4 road. You can follow this over to Kingston Peak, an easy walk a little over 1.0 mile from Lunch Rock.

GETTING THERE: The parking area for the standard route is off a paved road, but unfortunately, the lot is privately owned. A $5 parking fee is required to leave your vehicle at the lot (though there is no fee to enter the James Peak Wilderness).

There are two free trailheads you can start from if you want to avoid the parking fee, but you will miss out on the glacier (unless you hike down to it from above) and you'll need a 4x4, high-clearance vehicle to reach them. The first is Loch Lomond (page 122) which has a fine trail north from

James Peak's south slopes. "Lunch Rock" is the formation just right of center.

the Loch to James Peak and serves as a good base area if you want to hike Mount Bancroft and James Peak together, starting with Mount Bancroft.

The other parking area is up Mammoth Gulch. Mammoth Gulch Road spurs off East Portal Road (page 98) in the barely-there town of Tolland. This road is actually okay for sport utility cars like Subaru Outbacks if they stop at a large parking area about a mile below the upper parking area. From the East Portal Road in Tolland, follow Mammoth Gulch 4.0 miles uphill to the top of the road, then turn right onto the Kingston Peak 4x4 road and go 3.0 miles to the parking area. This route starts over Kingston Peak and then to James Peak.

Take Exit 238 off I-70 to Fall River Road and follow the paved road 8.6 miles along switchbacks and hills to the signed parking area on the west side of the road. You can't miss it, thanks to the dozens of signs bellowing the parking fee and the threat of getting towed.

THE ROUTE: The trail begins at the south side of the parking lot, up a wide dirt road with signs for the glacier. Not far into the hike, the road splits, going straight and left uphill. Head left and continue up the rocky road. In 0.7 mile you'll arrive at St. Marys Lake. The road/trail ends just after crossing a small bridge at the toe of the glacier.

Begin trekking up the glacier. This ascent is modestly steep—by Indian Peaks standards. For less-experienced hik-

On the St. Marys Glacier above St Marys Lake.

James Peak is a good autumn summit option.

ers, it can feel like a lot of work. Microspikes are a good idea for the shoulder seasons or for the added security of stable footing, although most summer ascents won't need them. Follow the glacier uphill to its source, where a trail will reappear above the last of the ice and snow.

Above the glacier, the hiking trail gradually blends into the terrain as you head toward a rock formation in the open tundra known as Lunch Rock. The first views of James Peak reveal the sheer size of its impressive domed summit. After 1.7 miles, arrive at Lunch Rock. One helpful exercise at this point is to look back at from where you came up from the glacier. There are two basins below from this point and each year, several hikers descend the wrong one. From Lunch Rock, continue about 1.0 mile west toward James Peak's east slopes.

At the foot of the peak, a hiking trail again appears, coming up from Loch Lomond. This trail heads up the east slopes, trending left of center. Follow the trail roughly 1.0 mile to the top of James Peak. When you reach the saddle between James Peak and Mount Bancroft, stay right (north) on the trail.

James Peak's summit is a broad, flat area with excellent 360-degree views. In the spring or early summer, you can save time on your descent by going directly down James' southeast ridge, which is easier to travel over when there is snow. Otherwise, you can retrace your steps on the way down. Remember when you reach the bottom of the slopes to aim for Lunch Rock, then be certain to aim left for the top of the glacier. Once there, enjoy the hike/slide back to St. Marys Lake and the way back to the parking area.

THE BEST INDIAN PEAKS WILDERNESS HIKES

19. Heart Lake and Heartbeat Peak

RATING	Moderate
ROUND-TRIP DISTANCE	8.5 miles Heart Lake (out-and-back); 11 miles Heartbeat Peak (out-and-back)
ROUND-TRIP TIME	4–6 hours Heart Lake; 5.5–7.5 hours Heartbeat Peak
ELEVATION GAIN	2,250 feet Heart Lake; 3,150 feet Heartbeat Peak
MAP	Trails Illustrated #103, Winter Park, Central City, Rollins Pass; Latitude 40° Maps - Front Range
NEAREST LANDMARK	Moffat Tunnel

COMMENT: This cardiac combo is an excellent way to enjoy a full day out starting at the East Portal trailhead. Rogers Pass Trail is a well-maintained route that allows for a quick pace up to Rogers Pass Lake. From there, the trail climbs up to Heart Lake (11,316 feet) and to Rogers Pass (11,900 feet). Atop Rogers Pass, the often-elusive Continental Divide Trail provides access to Heartbeat Peak, a fantastic summit on the eastern border of the James Peak Wilderness along the Continental Divide.

Unlike many summit hikes in the James Peak/Indian Peaks Wilderness areas, this one enjoys a prolonged prelude in the forest before breaking treeline. At 3.5 miles, the terrain transforms as you reach the lakes and eventually

THE BEST INDIAN PEAKS WILDERNESS HIKES

Along the trail after an unexpected summer snowstorm.

the high ridgeline. There are no technical sections or wild exposure, making this the ideal hike for those who want to focus on the details of nature's alpine transformation rather than route finding, scrambling, or challenging navigation.

Rogers Pass has gained favor with trail runners thanks to its relatively solid footing and gorgeous destinations. The oddball 4x4 road at Rogers Pass is an offshoot of the well-established western portion of Moffat Road that starts in Winter Park. Due to the closure of the Needle's Eye Tunnel, Moffat Road no longer connects to the eastern leg.

Heartbeat Peak (12,251 feet) is an unranked summit but still holds an impressive place along the Divide. One feature I like about Heart Lake: viewed from above, it resembles an actual human heart rather than a cartoony one.

GETTING THERE: From the town of Rollinsville off CO-119, turn west onto East Portal Road/Tolland Road. Follow this highly maintained dirt road 8.0 miles west to its terminus at the East Portal/Moffat Tunnel parking lot. This road is maintained year round and the parking lot is large. Trails begin to the right of the tunnel.

THE ROUTE: The Rogers Pass trailhead starts to the right of the tunnel at a signed trail. Your goal is simple: stay on this trail from here to Rogers Pass, 4.7 miles to the west. This is

Heart Lake with Heartbeat Peak in the distance.

Rogers Pass Lake.

a peaceful trail that gradually gains elevation, so it's never strenuous. Here are a few milestones to note en route to the pass: at 0.9 mile, junction with Forest Lakes Trail; at 1.6 miles, junction with Crater Lakes Trail; at 1.9 miles, junction with Clayton Lake Trail; at 3.6 miles, break treeline.

After 4.0 miles, you reach Rogers Pass Lake, the smaller of the two alpine lakes at 11,100 feet. From here, the trail gets steeper as it climbs 0.2 mile to Heart Lake, and then up to Rogers Pass. If Heart Lake was your goal for the day, relax and enjoy this accommodating lake at 11,315 feet and return the way you came when ready.

If heading up to Rogers Pass/Heartbeat Peak, push on up a series of steep switchbacks 0.5 mile to Rogers Pass. Unlike many mountain passes, the switchbacks to the pass are on a convex hillside versus a concave gully. At 11,950 feet, stand on the Continental Divide atop Rogers Pass. To the west is that … a road? Indeed, there is an old 4x4 road up here, as well as the Continental Divide Trail. Turn north and ascend 400 vertical feet in 0.8 mile to the summit of Heartbeat Peak, which looks more legit from this perspective. This rounded ridge holds potential for explorers who can traverse it north 3.7 miles all the way to Rollins Pass (often, this is done as part of a backpacking loop). Chances are you'll have had your fill getting to this point. Return the way you came along the Rogers Pass Trail.

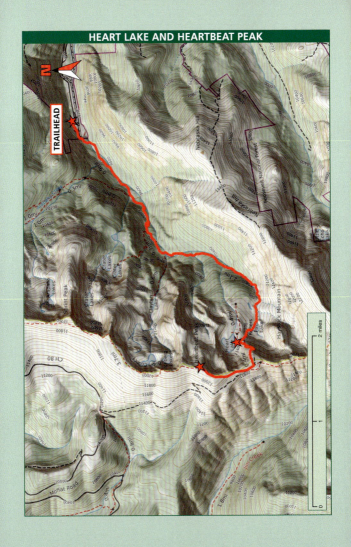

20. Crater Lakes

RATING	Easy
ROUND-TRIP DISTANCE	5.2 miles
ROUND-TRIP TIME	3–5 hours
ELEVATION GAIN	1,481 feet
MAP	Trails Illustrated #103, Winter Park, Central City, Rollins Pass; Latitude 40° Maps, Boulder County
NEAREST LANDMARK	Moffat Tunnel

COMMENT: The collection of lakes known as the Crater Lakes (10,580 feet) described here are accessed via the East Portal trailhead in the James Peak Wilderness (the other Crater Lake is on the west side of Pawnee Pass in the Indian Peaks Wilderness). This is a fun, casual outing that is a great hike in late spring or mid-autumn. It's actually a fun snowshoe in the winter, assuming you can find the trail. The two lower lakes are perfect for relaxing, enjoying a picnic, and taking in the views. Unlike most mountain hikes, you can start later in the day as the lower lakes are below treeline and storms aren't as big of a concern.

It's possible to scramble to the upper lakes if you're looking for a bit of solitude paired with a hearty hill climb. There are a lot of extras to enjoy on this relatively short hike, such as the drive in through the tiny town of Tolland, a look at the

Defiantly
unfrozen.

impressive East Portal Tunnel, and great views without a ton of effort.

The hike to Crater Lakes is a wonderful walk in the woods, though the trail can get a little busy in the summer. October to December is my favorite time of the year to visit, when there's a dusting of snow on the ground and a rim of thin ice around the lakes. Protected from the elements, these lakes are an alpine sanctuary surrounded by rugged wilderness. More than once I've hiked up with a portable hammock, a good book, and my dogs and spent a few hours simply "being" in the mountains.

The drive to the trailhead on East Portal Road is a destination in itself. Small cabins, an old schoolhouse, train tracks, open meadows, mountain views, and a roadside river set a Rocky Mountain scene that is pure Colorado. Note that this access road is part of the old Moffat Road, which is covered in the Needle's Eye Tunnel Hike on page 97.

The Crater Lakes are neatly tucked into the trees.

Bridge crossing lower on the trail.

GETTING THERE: From the town of Rollinsville off CO-119, turn west onto East Portal Road/Tolland Road. Follow this highly maintained dirt road 8.0 miles west to its terminus at the East Portal/Moffat Tunnel parking lot. This road is maintained year round and the parking lot is large. Trails begin to the right of the tunnel.

THE ROUTE: The trail begins on the northwest side of the lot and bypasses Moffat Tunnel as it heads into the forest. At times, this parking lot can be home to ballistic winds but often the winds completely disappear when you go into the woods. After 1.2 miles, in a spacious meadow, the trail continues straight at a junction with the Forest Lakes Trail.

Continue 0.6 mile and turn right onto Crater Lakes Trail. It's 0.9 mile to the lakes from here and you'll gain 600 vertical feet along the way. These lower twin lakes are popular camping spots, thanks in part to their sheltered location below treeline on a flat shelf of land. Scrambling up to the upper lakes (there are no trails) is a bonus option for those who want to get above treeline. Return back the way you came.

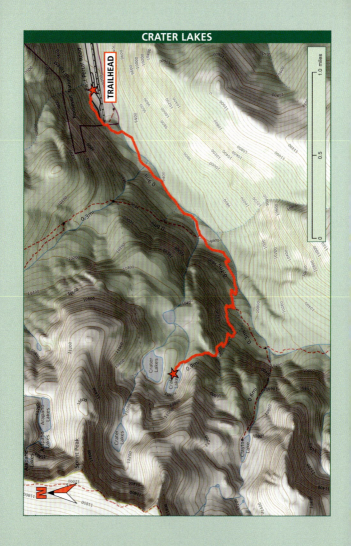

TRAILHEAD

21. Mount Bancroft and Parry Peak

RATING	Moderate
ROUND-TRIP DISTANCE	5.3 miles
ROUND-TRIP TIME	5–6 hours
ELEVATION GAIN	2,760 feet
MAP	Trails Illustrated #103, Winter Park, Central City, Rollins Pass; Latitude 40° Maps - Front Range
NEAREST LANDMARK	Fall River Road

COMMENT: This dynamic duo trek passes by two beautiful lakes—Loch Lomond and Lake Caroline (11,896 feet)—before tackling the rocky slopes up Mount Bancroft (13,250 feet). An easy traverse connects Bancroft to Parry Peak (13,391 feet) the highest point in the James Peak Wilderness. There are faint trails to both summits, but no formal trail beyond the remnants of an old 4x4 road up to Lake Caroline. That said, the navigation here is easy and the mountain views are spectacular.

Parry Peak is named for Charles Parry (1823–1890), a botanist who had plenty of influence naming many of the peaks in the area. Mount Eva (page 126) he named after his wife and he also named James Peak, Grays Peak, Torreys Peak, and Engelmann Peak for fellow botanists. Not surprisingly, he also named Mount Flora (page 130). Mount Bancroft, however, is named for Dr. Frederick Bancroft (1834–1903), an early Colorado doctor. Lake Caroline is named for his daughter (1900–1985), who earned some renown for her role in the *Ziegfield Follies*.

GETTING THERE: You will need a high-clearance 4x4 SUV to make this trailhead. From I-70, take Exit 238 onto Fall River Road and follow it north 8.3 miles to the tiny town of Alice. Turn left onto Alice Road and follow it 0.9 mile up a steep portion of the road and turn right onto Steuart Road. The road is signed along with a sign for Loch Lomond.

From here, it's 2.3 miles to Loch Lomond. In recent years, this road has taken a beating. As recently as 2015, the road was passable by sport utility cars. Thanks to deep ruts and more rocks than ever, you'll need an SUV with good clearance to reach the trailhead.

Looking at the ridge to James Peak from Mount Bancroft.

Bounce up, climbing a few steep hills, before reaching the popular, large parking area for Loch Lomond.

THE ROUTE: Start south, away from Loch Lemond, up the 4x4 road. Follow it as it climbs 0.6 mile into the basin below Bancroft's east slopes. When the road heads up the ridge, stay low in the basin. The easiest way to gain the southeast ridge is farther along, past Lake Caroline (on your right), then up the lowest angle slopes to gain the ridge. The 4x4 road fizzles

Traversing from Bancroft to Parry Peak.

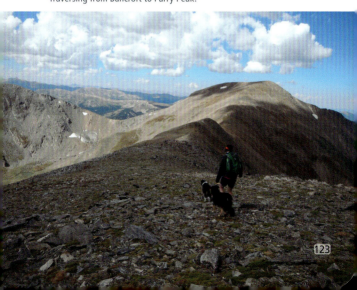

Classic summit cairn.   Mount Eva in the distance.

out the higher you go and you may see faint casual trails to the ridge.

After 1.3 miles, at 12,600 feet, gain Bancroft's southeast ridge and continue up to the summit. There are some Class 2 boulder fields to navigate—staying left tends to offer grassier, easier terrain.

From the summit, the walk over to Parry Peak is obvious via a ridge to the west. Footing is excellent and the walk over to the higher of the two peaks is a casual affair. In less than 1.0 mile you'll be standing on the highest ground in the James Peak Wilderness. Return the way you came, via Bancroft and the southeast ridge. A detour to Lake Caroline is a nice option on the way down.

Easy terrain on the traverse between the peaks.

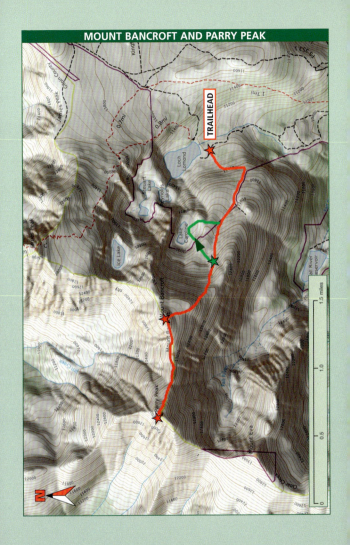

TRAILHEAD

22. Mount Eva and Witter Peak

RATING	Difficult
ROUND-TRIP DISTANCE	4.7 miles
ROUND-TRIP TIME	5–7 hours
ELEVATION GAIN	2,225 feet
MAP	Trails Illustrated #103, Winter Park, Central City, Rollins Pass, Latitude 40° Maps - Front Range
NEAREST LANDMARK	Fall River Road

COMMENT: Mount Eva (13,130 feet) is the lowest of the five 13ers in the James Peak Wilderness but may very well have the best summit views. The terrain to the top is a mix of lakes, marshes, willows, and talus—all of it off trail. The difficulty never exceeds Class 2 and the navigation is straightforward. This basin is one of the most beautiful in the James Peak Wilderness. The trio of lakes at the start gives way to flowery, grassy meadows that decorate the slopes all the way to the summit.

Witter Peak (12,884 feet) is a secondary summit and is included as part of the standard route here. From the saddle between Witter and Eva, the hike up to Witter is nearly flat. Witter's south face is framed with dramatic and steep cliffs. Hiking off Witter's southeast ridge has a few interesting Class 2+ scrambles before slopes lead back into the basin and to Chinns Lake.

Don't let the off-trail character of this hike deter you. Navigation is straightforward and nearly all above treeline. The basin above Chinns Lake is known for its large patches of colorful wildflowers and deep green willows, thanks to the abundance of creeks and streams.

GETTING THERE: You will need a high-clearance vehicle with 4WD to reach this trailhead. It is possible to make it up with a carefully driven sport utility car with good clearance like a

On the way to Witter after summiting Mount Eva.

RAV4 or Honda CRV, but it's better to take an SUV. Passenger cars can bounce their way up about 2.0 miles of the 3.4-mile road, though they may take some damage

From I-70, take Exit 238 onto Fall River Road. Stay on Fall River Road 6.6 miles to a sharp hairpin turn. Exit Fall River Road and take the dirt 4x4 road here (called Rainbow Road on some maps) and follow the signs toward Chinns Lake. This road is rutted, rocky, and should be driven with care. Stay on the main 4x4 road 2.4 miles to a signed split for Fall River Reservoir and Chinns Lake. Stay left and proceed 1.1 miles to Chinns Lake, where parking is plentiful.

THE ROUTE: Start from the end of the road on the west side of Chinns Lake. There are a few casual trails around the lake and through the woods, including one that heads up to Slater Lake. Take it or forge your own way 0.2 mile, but find your way to Slater Lake.

From Slater Lake, head up through the heart of the basin toward the large saddle at the west end. Most of the footing here is surprisingly solid, though you'll be forced to find your way through a brief section of marshy, tall willows. These can be somewhat avoided by staying right (north) in the basin.

Mount Eva from the south.

Fun scrambles descending Witter Peak.

After that, keep pushing up, first on grassy slopes, then on loose, rocky dirt to the saddle.

After 1.5 miles, at 12,750 feet, you reach the saddle between Eva and Witter. Head north to Eva's summit on good, solid slopes. Near the top, you'll encounter the ruins of an old radio tower and cabin. Even though it's only 2.0 miles, you'll have earned this summit! It's a broad, open plateau with a very shoddy wind shelter. From here the walk over to Witter is very obvious and easy. Return to the saddle and keep rolling.

The most direct way back is to scramble down Witter's east ridge past a short section of fun downclimbing (Class 2+), and then hit the slopes north, back into the basin and back to Chinns Lake. While these slopes are a little bit steep, the footing is solid, mostly on grassy tufts with a few embedded boulders.

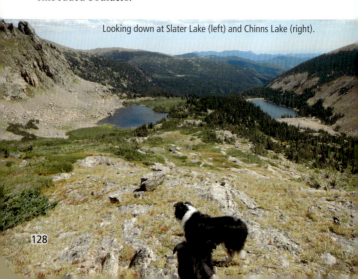
Looking down at Slater Lake (left) and Chinns Lake (right).

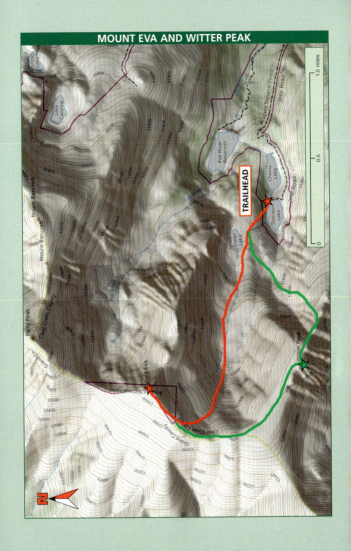

TRAILHEAD

N

23. Mount Flora

RATING	Moderate
ROUND-TRIP DISTANCE	6.4 miles
ROUND-TRIP TIME	3–5 hours
ELEVATION GAIN	1,800 feet Mount Flora
MAP	Trails Illustrated #103, Winter Park, Central City, Rollins Pass; Latitude 40° Maps - Front Range
NEAREST LANDMARK	Berthoud Pass

COMMENT: Mount Flora (13,146 feet) is an excellent Class 2 hike to a ranked 13er. The Mount Flora Trail connects with the Continental Divide, offering expansive views in all directions. Included in the tour is a look at the old Berthoud Pass ski area and the high-tech array of radio towers on neighboring Colorado Mines Peak. Berthoud Pass itself twists into Winter Park below, while the far-off summits of the Indian Peaks loom north on the horizon.

Along the Mount Flora Trail.

Colorado Mines Peak.

Mount Flora is a fantastic option for casual hikers who are looking for a high-reward day with a modest amount of work. Experienced mountain trekkers will also appreciate the classic Colorado scenery along with the option to tag three summits in a single outing (Colorado Mines Peak and Breckenridge Peak). Because of the high-elevation start, this hike is accessible year round, although winter's heavy snow brings an avalanche risk.

GETTING THERE: Take I-70 to Exit 232 to US-40 toward Empire. Stay on US-40 for 14.8 miles up the paved, switchbacking road to the top of Berthoud Pass. There is a large parking area on the right, complete with a restroom and informational hut.

THE ROUTE: Start up the wide road on the southeast side of the lot. Stay on this road up a few switchbacks. Elevation gain is gradual and a nice 0.8-mile prelude before getting off the road and onto the Mount Flora Trail. Head north along the well-made trail with the occasional rocky section. Eventually, it meets up with the ridge along the Continental Divide and continues north.

The ridge can get windy!　　　　Summit of Mount Flora.

At 2.3 miles, Point 12,805 is an unnamed summit en route to Mount Flora. The trail continues north to Mount Flora, which now cuts a mammoth profile along the ridge. The hike up Flora's southwest slopes may require very light, easy scrambling. In another 0.9 mile, reach the summit at 13,146 feet. Enjoy your time on this venerable summit, then return the way you came.

Breckenridge Peak and Colorado Mines Peak: From the summit of Flora, it's 0.8 mile southeast to 12,889-foot Breckenridge Peak. It's an easy side-trip on Class 2, off-trail terrain. Another obvious option is to walk up to Colorado Mines Peak, 12,493-feet, only 0.3 mile from the saddle where the Mount Flora Trail meets the Continental Divide.

If you feel like going big, it's possible to hike the Continental Divide northeast to James Peak (page 110)—and beyond! A traverse from Berthoud Pass to James Peak is roughly 13.2 miles and covers 5 to 6 mountains: Colorado Mines Peak (if you opt for it), Mount Flora, Mount Eva, Parry Peak, Mount Bancroft, and James Peak.

Great views on the return hike from Mount Flora.

TRAILHEAD

1.5 miles

1.0

0.5

0

24. Colorado Mines Peak and Hidden Point

RATING	Easy
ROUND-TRIP DISTANCE	4 miles (loop)
ROUND-TRIP TIME	2.5–3.5 hours
ELEVATION GAIN	1,306 feet
MAP	Trails Illustrated #103, Winter Park, Central City, Rollins Pass; Latitude 40° Maps - Front Range
NEAREST LANDMARK	Berthoud Pass

COMMENT: This wonderful tour off Berthoud Pass packs a lot of adventure into a compact, enjoyable hike. The obvious star of the show is Colorado Mines Peak (12,493 feet), once the top of ski lifts that serviced the now-defunct Berthoud Ski Area. Reaching its summit arrayed with buildings and towers is a novelty, but there's a secret destination before you reach this highest point.

Southeast of Colorado Mines Peak is a small, humble micro-summit known as Hidden Point (11,988 feet). It's really just an anomalous rock pile on the shoulder of its par-

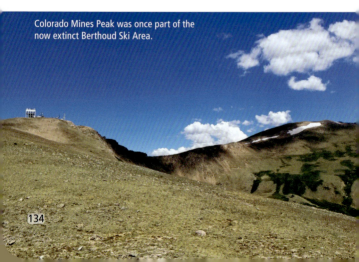

Colorado Mines Peak was once part of the now extinct Berthoud Ski Area.

This thin trail materializes from the grassy tundra as you near Hidden Point.

ent peak, but its relative isolation and stunning scenery are worth a look. To the north of this point is 12,255-foot Cone Mountain (page 138). To the south, past the deep cut valley where I-70 runs, is the impressive north face of 13,362-foot Engelmann Peak. Even though there is a bit of off-trail tundra walking, this is an easy hike that can be made longer by walking north along the Continental Divide.

GETTING THERE: Take I-70 to Exit 232 to US-40 toward Empire. Stay on US-40 for 14.8 miles up the paved, switchbacking road to the top of Berthoud Pass. There is a large parking area on the right, complete with a restroom and informational hut.

THE ROUTE: From the busy parking lot, begin your hike on a wide access road at the southeast side of the lot. Don't worry, you won't be on it long. In 0.2 mile, at a switchback in the road, a mysterious, unsigned trail beckons into the forest. This improvised path only goes through the woods a short distance before reaching the open tundra en route to your first goal, Hidden Point. Take this shady trail. (If you prefer a little less woodsy travel, you can stay on the road up another two switchbacks, then hop off the road up higher—it will be all out of the trees with this option.)

The summit of Colorado Mines Peak.

After 0.5 mile, at 11,290 feet, the trail pops out of the woods and disappears ... for a while. No worries! Simply keep trending uphill to the east, aiming for a flat portion south of the road and Colorado Mines Peak. Off-trail navigation doesn't get much easier than this. Views are incredible and the sense of isolation adds to the beauty of the day. In another 0.5 mile, at 11,950 feet, a new trail materializes from the tundra and is surprisingly well traveled. Follow this nifty alpine path 0.4 mile to an obvious terminus at a small, rocky perch.

Hidden Point is a great place to sit, relax, and watch the world go by. It has a wonderfully detached view of the traffic down on I-70 along with plenty of mountain vistas. From here, the walk up to Colorado Mines Peak is an easy tundra trek due north.

Colorado Mines Peak is an interesting summit. It's home to a host of radio towers, bunker-like buildings, and some relics from its days as a ski area. Even though this hike is an easy circuit, it's quite rewarding. Seeing the mountain terrain mixed with man-made highways and structures is an impressive contrast.

If you're feeling scrappy, it's possible to hike north to the saddle off Colorado Mines Peak, then east down to shimmering Blue Lake. This side journey is only 0.5 mile off the summit but drops—and regains—900 vertical feet!

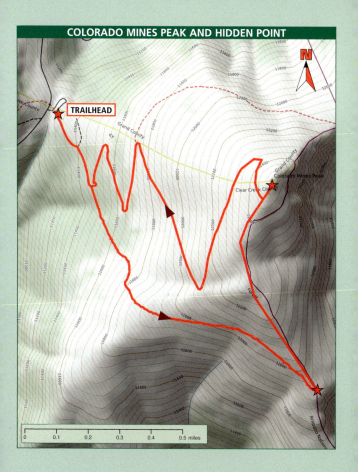

TRAILHEAD

Grand County

Grand County
Colorado Mines Peak
Clear Creek County

N

0   0.1   0.2   0.3   0.4   0.5 miles

25. Cone Mountain

RATING	Moderate
ROUND-TRIP DISTANCE	7.1 miles
ROUND-TRIP TIME	4–6 hours
ELEVATION GAIN	2,200 feet
MAP	Trails Illustrated #103, Winter Park, Central City, Rollins Pass; Latitude 40° Maps - Front Range
NEAREST LANDMARK	Berthoud Pass

COMMENT: Cone Mountain (12,224 feet) is a hidden gem that doesn't see many visitors. Cone is the southern-most summit in the James Peak Wilderness, thus the southern-most peak in this guide. You'll have to hike downhill from the Continental Divide along boulder-riddled slopes to reach this peak, though the final walk to the top is on accommodating, less rocky terrain. Views west from Cone's summit of Colorado Mines Peak and the Continental Divide offer a unique vantage of the rolling ridge.

The start of this hike follows the same trail as Mount Flora (page 130), although the two don't make for a great combo

Start up the Mount Flora Trail.

Not many people visit Cone Mountain. Note the curious rock lines.

due to the up-and-down required to get to both summits. One option from Cone, however, is to visit Blue Lake below Colorado Mines Peak on the return.

Despite having a few miles of off-trail navigation, it's along obvious ridges and above treeline. Route finding is easy, the challenge is in lining up the best footing.

GETTING THERE: Take I-70 to Exit 232 to US-40 toward Empire. Stay on US-40 for 14.8 miles up the paved, switchbacking road to the top of Berthoud Pass. There is a large parking area on the right, complete with a restroom and informational hut.

THE ROUTE: From the Berthoud Pass parking area, start on the wide road at the southeast side of the lot. Stay on this road for 0.8 mile. Hop on the signed Mount Flora Trail and continue another 0.8 mile to a saddle where the trail meets the ridge.

At the saddle, you have options. Cone Mountain stands to the east and the most direct path is to get off trail north of the saddle and begin a straight shot to the flat saddle west of Cone Mountain. The footing this way is passable but loose in places. Time-wise, it may be just as effective to hike higher

Go off-trail east of the Mount Flora Trail.

Some of the on-trail hiking.

and descend the connecting ridge from the Continental Divide—the next few steps will describe this option. Stay on the Mount Flora Trail for 0.8 mile to Point 12,805.

From here, stay on the ridge that breaks off southeast toward Peak 12,845. It's tricky to stay on the top of the ridge due to large boulders and spotty footing. To the right of the ridge on the slopes has slightly better footing and spares you the trouble of ascending to Peak 12,845 if you'd prefer to bypass it. Eventually, level off in a flat section before the last push up to Cone Mountain.

At 12,140 feet you're almost there. There are several interesting rock patterns, seemingly man-made, throughout this alpine field. Continue a short distance to the summit of Cone Mountain. Congratulations on visiting one of the most overlooked James Peak Wilderness mountains.

The easiest way to return is to angle directly toward the saddle above Blue Lake near Colorado Mines Peak. After about 1.6 miles, regain the ridge and the Mount Flora Trail and follow it back to the parking lot.

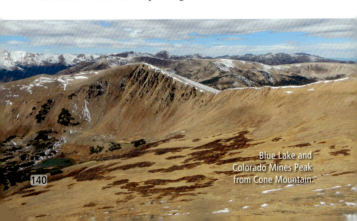

Blue Lake and Colorado Mines Peak from Cone Mountain.

TRAILHEAD

Cone Mountain

About the Author

James Dziezynski is the author of two other Colorado guide-books, *Best Summit Hikes in Colorado* and *Best Summit Hikes: Denver to Vail*. James studied literature and philosophy at Marist College and is a graduate of NOLS, the National Outdoor Leadership School. His writing has appeared in *National Geographic Adventure, Discover Magazine, Outside, Backpacker, Elevation Outdoors, The Denver Post,* and many other print and online publications.

James lives in Boulder with his wife Sheila and their two rescue dogs, Mystic and Fremont. He's climbed over 1,000 Colorado summits including all of Colorado's 14ers as well as summiting all the legally accessible named summits in the Indian Peaks and James Peak Wilderness areas.

Checklist

The Best Indian Peaks Wilderness Hikes

☐	Hike 1	St. Vrain Mountain and Meadow Mountain
☐	Hike 2	Watanga Lake and Watanga Mountain
☐	Hike 3	Hiamovi Mountain and Mount Irving Hale
☐	Hike 4	Gourd Lake
☐	Hike 5	Crater Lake
☐	Hike 6	Mount Neva and Mount Jasper
☐	Hike 7	Sawtooth Mountain
☐	Hike 8	Pawnee Pass Area
☐	Hike 9	Mount Audubon and Paiute Peak
☐	Hike 10	Little Pawnee Peak
☐	Hike 11	Blue Lake
☐	Hike 12	Navajo Peak
☐	Hike 13	Arapaho Peaks
☐	Hike 14	Lake Dorothy
☐	Hike 15	Needle's Eye Tunnel
☐	Hike 16	Bob and Betty Lakes
☐	Hike 17	Diamond Lake
☐	Hike 18	James Peak
☐	Hike 19	Heart Lake and Heartbeat Peak
☐	Hike 20	Crater Lakes
☐	Hike 21	Mount Bancroft and Parry Peak
☐	Hike 22	Mount Eva and Witter Peak
☐	Hike 23	Mount Flora
☐	Hike 24	Colorado Mines Peak and Hidden Point
☐	Hike 25	Cone Mountain

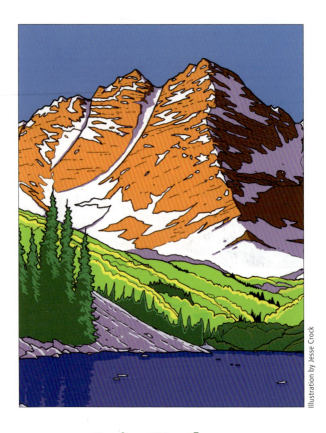

Illustration by Jesse Crock

Join Today.
Adventure Tomorrow.

The Colorado Mountain Club helps you maximize living in an outdoor playground and connects you with other adventure-loving mountaineers. We summit 14ers, climb rock faces, work to protect the mountain experience, and educate generations of Coloradans.